FUNDING YOUR FUTURE

The book that the experts recommend!

"A BOOK INVESTORS HAVE BEEN WAITING FOR."
  —Kenneth S. Janke, president & CEO, National Association of Investors Corporation

"PACKED WITH GOOD ADVICE . . . will help both new and experienced mutual fund investors achieve their financial dreams."
  —Jonathan D. Pond, editor, *Wiesenberger Mutual Funds Investment Report*

"EASY TO READ AND TO UNDERSTAND. . . . AN EXCELLENT JOB."
  —James B. Cloonan, chairman, American Association of Individual Investors

"A MUST-READ FOR ALL THOSE WHO WISH TO GROW RICH SAFELY . . . offers valuable information to everyone, from the novice investor to the seasoned mutual fund jockey. Jonathan Clements shows how even the most conservative investor can profit, suggesting several sample portfolios, which include the nation's best—and lowest-cost—performers."
  —Alyssa A. Lappen, money editor, *Working Woman* magazine

"CONCISE, UNDERSTANDABLE, AND TO THE POINT . . . a great book for the vast majority of American investors—those who want to invest some money, leave it alone for years, and get on with the really enjoyable things in life . . . just the book my listeners have been asking for."
  —Don McDonald, "The Don McDonald Show," Business Radio Network

FUNDING YOUR FUTURE

The Only Guide to Mutual Funds You'll Ever Need

JONATHAN CLEMENTS

WARNER BOOKS

A Time Warner Company

Warner Books, Inc., 1271 Avenue of the Americas, New York, NY 10020

 A Time Warner Company

Printed in the United States of America
First Printing: November 1993
10 9 8 7 6 5 4 3 2

Library of Congress Cataloging-in-Publication Data

Clements, Jonathan.
    Funding your future : the only guide to mutual funds you'll ever need / Jonathan Clements.
        p. cm.
    Includes index.
    ISBN 0-446-39496-3
    1. Mutual funds.   I. Title.
HG4530.C49   1993
332.63'27—dc20   92-46627
                                                          CIP

Cover design by Christine Van Blee
Book design by L. McRee

For Molly

Contents

Preface

W*all Street Journal* readers have a peculiar perception
that *Journal* reporters are both financial experts and
public servants. My daily stack of mail often includes
a lengthy letter begging for advice on how to invest in mutual
funds. Every day brings a few calls from readers requesting
toll-free telephone numbers for this or that fund group. Invariably these requests balloon into a slew of other questions. Along the way, I learn the intimate details of a total
stranger's financial life. Some callers even ask for a "hot"
fund tip, as though there were some magical fund that would
answer all their investment prayers.

All this contact with the investing public brought with it a
disturbing revelation: In my articles, I was clearly failing to
answer a lot of basic questions that *Journal* readers had. So,
on a blistering hot July morning in 1991, dodging the traffic
as I made my way to the *Journal*'s Manhattan headquarters,
it dawned on me that I should write a series of easy-to-
understand articles on how to pick a mutual fund.

Ten days later, the first of five articles appeared. Reader response was overwhelming. That first day, and in the days that followed, my telephone went haywire. It rang so frequently and my days were so consumed with fielding reader inquiries that I had to scramble to complete the series on schedule. Then came a second series in late September, that one on putting together a mutual fund portfolio. Again, my phone went berserk.

In response to the two series, I received dozens of letters. A few were critical, like the one that began, "Poo, your retirement funding advice sucks bilge water." Most, however, were complimentary and some were downright endearing.

A reader from the Pacific rim sent a note, badly typed and entirely in capital letters: "I HAV' A MOS' IMPORTANT QUESTION WHICH I COULDN'T DEDUCT FROM YOUR ARTICLES; SHOULD A PERSON HAVE, SAY, $100,000, WHERE SHOULD HE INVEST IT FOR GROWTH. THERE ARE AT LEAST SIX HUNDRED MUTUAL FUNDS OUT THERE, WITH SO MANY EXPERTS. HOW CAN ONE COMPETE AGAINST ALL THAT? I REALIZE THIS IS ASK'G MUCH. BUT I'M STUMP, EVEN AFTER READ'G YOUR ARTICLES. PLEAS' HELP. THANKU."

Then there was the hapless undergraduate who read some of my articles, decided to skip mutual funds, and instead plunged directly into the stock market. By a series of missteps, he ended up buying stock in one of the most embattled companies listed on the New York Stock Exchange. "I thought I was the biggest chump on the face of the earth," he wrote. "Fortunately, the stock has stabilized (I think), and I will wait for about two months before selling the stock."

The huge response to my two series convinced me that I should write a book on mutual funds. In putting together this book, the reader I imagined most often was the novice investor who sent me this letter shortly after my second series appeared: "I am interested in getting started in the stock and bond market but am completely lost. It seems as though everyone around me knows exactly how everything works and assumes I do as well. I am too embarrassed to ask someone for help and have turned to you. Is there a pamphlet, booklet, or something available to people who wish to start in the market? I don't really want to go to a stockbroker right away either because I will feel stupid. Could you please advise me where to look for information, or give me some suggestions. I don't even have a clue as to how much money I need to really get started, or how to find a good stockbroker, if you even need one, or how much they take for commission, and how to find a good stock."

With this in mind, I have tried to write this book so that it is comprehensible to those who have no knowledge of mutual funds or the securities markets. If there is anything in this book that readers cannot readily understand, it is not the fault of their comprehension but a failure of my powers of explanation. While I have tried to make this book as straightforward as possible, I have also sought to avoid oversimplification. In other words, I do not ignore or gloss over key areas of investing just because they are complex.

Within these pages is everything that I believe an investor needs to put together a complete investment program. For those setting out to save for retirement or for their children's college educations, or for those struggling to maintain a decent standard of living in retirement, I hope *Funding Your Future* will be a worthy companion.

Dozens of people helped with the writing of this book. I inflicted the manuscript on a number of current and former journalistic colleagues, including John Dorfman, Laura Jereski, Robert McGough, Gay Miller, Ronit Addis Rose, and Frederic Wiegold.

I also sought the advice of mutual fund experts such as Robert Bingham, Richard Fried, Kenneth Gregory, A. Michael Lipper, Craig Litman, Ron Olin, Gerald Perritt, and Don Phillips. The mutual fund industry's two preeminent research firms, Lipper Analytical Services, Inc., and Morningstar, Inc., kindly agreed to let me use their data.

I even managed to impose on a good number of family members, including Nicholas Clements, Richard Clements, June Dosik, Richard Dosik, Alice Greene, and Lydia Greene. These were my guinea pigs, who could tell me if the book was intelligible to the amateur investor.

Publishing has always struck me as a capricious business. But with this book I was fortunate enough to work with three consummate professionals, my agent, Dan Green, and my two editors at Warner Books, Rick Horgan and Susan Suffes. Their insights and encouragement undoubtedly made this a better book.

Funding Your Future is dedicated to my wife, Molly, with good reason. In a year when we bought a house, had a second child, and Molly both finished her Ph.D. and landed an academic job, she still gave me the time to write this book. I am profoundly grateful.

☐PART I☐
FUNDING YOUR FUTURE WITH STOCK MUTUAL FUNDS

1

Taking Stock: Why Every Investor Should Be in the Stock Market

L et's face it—when it comes to investing, Americans are doing a pretty lousy job.

You want proof? Take a look at the baby boomers, that angst-ridden group of people born between 1946 and 1964. These folks are a sorry sight—if you look at their wallets. A 1990 study conducted for the Investment Company Institute, the trade group for the mutual fund industry, found that the average household headed by baby boomers had savings of just $37,000. In truth, the typical household probably has far less than that; such averages tend to be distorted by the huge sums of wealth held by a privileged few. More alarming still, only 12% of that $37,000 was in stocks or stock mutual funds. The bulk of the money, fully 71%, was in ultrasafe investments, such as savings accounts, bonds, money market funds, and bank certificates of deposit (CDs).

What is the chance that these folks are going to retire in comfort or pay for their children's college educations without going deeply into debt? Perilously slim. University tuition costs are soaring. Traditional sources of retirement income, such as company pensions and Social Security, are unlikely to provide more than a small portion of the money that many baby boomers will need to sustain their lifestyles after they leave the workforce. Instead, as retirees, they will have to rely heavily on their own savings, especially money stashed away in things like Individual Retirement Accounts and company retirement programs like profit-sharing plans and 401(k) plans.

The fact is that we are all becoming increasingly responsible for our own financial futures. How are we holding up under the pressure? Not too well, if the results of the Investment Company Institute study are anything to judge by. Explaining this behavior isn't easy. Maybe it's a lack of education about money, or perhaps a lack of self-discipline. But whatever the reason, it is clear not only that we are saving too little but that much of what we are squirreling away is ending up in ridiculously safe investments that will deliver lousy long-term results.

If you are seeking a secure financial future, now is the time to begin investing intelligently. For starters, consider one extremely uncomfortable fact: Unless you are wealthy or content to while away your retirement years in poverty, you must begin investing heavily in stocks or stock mutual funds. For many people, the very idea is terrifying. Bewildered by the stock market's gyrations and consumed by the fear that their money will be devoured in a stock market crash, they cling fervently to such conservative investments as bond funds, bank certificates of deposit, and money market funds. But in fact, stocks are far less risky than these other investments—if you properly understand risk.

Choosing Between Two Evils

For investors, there are two key risks: volatility and inflation. Volatility—the daily ups and downs of the stock market—can rattle even the most experienced investors. But volatility is a short-term problem, one that can be cured by the passage of time. As long as you have the tenacity to hang on, stock prices will eventually recover and go higher, and what at the time seemed like a major market calamity turns out later to be only a minor hiccup.

The fear of a stock market crash stops many investors from ever venturing into the market. But if you set up an investment program where you are putting money into the stock market on a regular basis—say, every month or every three months—then it is possible to view stock market swings with far greater equanimity. Every time the market rises, you get a little richer. Every time the market falls, you know your next investment will be buying shares at a lower price.

While stock market volatility is cured by time, inflation is a threat that is unlikely ever to go away. Once the real value of your savings has been eaten away by inflation, the only immediate cure is to replenish your capital by saving a lot more money. For those who are retired, this may not be an option.

It is inflation that makes bond funds, money market funds, and bank certificates of deposit so risky. These savings vehicles are often known as "fixed income" investments, because they kick off a relatively safe and predictable stream of income. For instance, if you buy a $1,000 bond that will pay 5% for 15 years, you know exactly what you will get: Every year for 15 years you will receive $50 and, provided you hold it to its full maturity of 15 years, you will get back your original $1,000 investment.

That safety and predictability are no doubt comforting. But they also come at a steep price. Fixed income investments do a lackluster job of generating inflation-beating returns. All a money market fund or a CD investor gets back is his original investment, plus interest. Bond investors suffer a similar fate. If you own bonds, the bulk of your gain comes from the interest kicked off by the bonds. In addition, you may reap some capital gains, which come from rising bond prices, but you are just as likely to suffer a capital loss. Bonds, after all, are generally redeemed at the same price at which they were originally issued.

Stock funds, by contrast, share in the growth of the economy and thus can earn handsome capital gains over time. Stock funds also benefit because many corporations regularly raise the quarterly dividends they pay to their shareholders. Although $1,000 invested in a bond fund or a money market fund will probably generate more immediate income than $1,000 put into a stock fund, over time the stock fund is likely to post far better returns, because it will benefit from both capital gains and rising dividends. Those capital gains show up both in a stock fund's rising share price and in the capital gains "distributions" that stock funds usually pay out to shareholders each year.

Cutting the Bonds, Getting Your Share

In recent years, much has been made of the unusually high stock market returns of the 1980s, when stock funds earned an average 15.5% a year, comfortably ahead of the 5.1% annual inflation rate. The pundits have warned—correctly—that stock fund investors shouldn't expect those sorts of returns in the future.

. Far less has been made of the wonderful gains that have gone to bond fund investors over the same period. According to Lipper Analytical Services, taxable bond mutual funds returned 11.1% annually through the 1980s. Just as investors shouldn't be misled by the fabulous stock fund returns of the 1980s, so they shouldn't be deceived by the rich bond fund gains. Neither stocks nor bonds are likely to do nearly as well in the years ahead.

So what sorts of returns can you expect? According to Chicago's Ibbotson Associates, stocks have returned about

7 percentage points a year more than inflation since 1926, and corporate and government bonds about 2 percentage points more. These are so-called total return numbers, which means that they reflect not only the gain or loss in security prices but also the effect of reinvesting any interest and dividend income kicked off by the securities.

Just as the results of the 1980s may make bonds look too good, so the Ibbotson data may do bonds an injustice. The bond market has now become better attuned to the faster pace of inflation that has existed since the mid-1960s. Over the past 20 years, for instance, corporate and government bonds have delivered around 3 percentage points a year more than inflation. Many investment advisers expect that those sorts of bond returns will persist in the future.

But even with a 3% annual return above inflation and despite their greater safety, bonds still seem a poor alternative to stocks, with their historical postinflation return of 7%. The difference between 3% and 7% may seem slight, and indeed it is, if you look only at 1 or 2 years. But over time, those small differences translate into big sums of money, because of the way compounding works.

Compounding is the process by which money is multiplied, so that in any one year you make money not only on your original investment but also on the gains achieved in earlier years. Thus, if you invest $100 and earn 7%, you would have $107 at the end of the first year. If you leave all your gains in the market, and keep earning 7% every year, you will have $114.49 at the end of 2 years, $122.50 at the end of 3 years, and $196.72 at the end of 10 years. At 7% a year, the value of your money will double every 10 years or so. But at 3% a year, the compounding process slows to a crawl, so that it takes more than 23 years to double your money. If you are 20 years old and stash away some money in stocks, you could expect its real, inflation-adjusted value to grow 21-fold by the time you turn 65. But with bonds, your money wouldn't even quadruple.

Of course, stocks and bonds don't outpace inflation every year by 7 and 3 percentage points, respectively. Over the short term, results can vary wildly from the long-term averages, especially if you are a stock investor. Since World War II, stocks have returned as much as 52.6% in a calendar year and lost as much as 26.5%. But over long time periods—10, 15, 20 years—the long-term historical averages are more likely to prevail, with stocks comfortably beating bonds.

The Secret of Your Success

This book's principal aim is to show you how to invest in stock mutual funds in a systematic and logical manner. The approach described here won't stop the value of your portfolio from ebbing and flowing with every stock market swing, nor will it allow you to make a fast buck. Instead, this book is intended for the patient investor who is looking to invest for 10 years or longer. What this book attempts to do is provide an intelligent approach to the stock market that should—over the long run—have a high probability of success. That high probability doesn't come from any magic formulas or madcap trading strategies. Rather, it is dependent on the simple notion that stocks deliver superior returns over the long haul. Thus, if your portfolio does at least as well as the stock market, and hopefully somewhat better, then you should end up with superior returns.

How heavily should you invest in stocks? You ought to have at least a modest amount of emergency money tucked away in safe, conservative investments. Some investment advisers suggest keeping emergency money equal to six months' living expenses, although you may find you are comfortable holding far less than that amount.

Apart from some emergency money, it is probably wise for most investors—except those who are retired or within 10 years of retirement—to have their investment portfolio largely or even entirely in stocks, providing they can be fairly sure that they won't have to cash in their portfolio at short notice. For those in retirement, keeping at least half their portfolio in stocks is probably prudent.

Prudent? To many, that sort of commitment to stocks might seem like banking your life savings on a weekend in Vegas. But the fact is that the principal key to investment success is to ensure that you minimize your holdings of bonds and similar poor-performing investments and maximize your position in stocks. Just by doing that you greatly enhance your chances of retiring comfortably or sending young Hannah to Harvard. Indeed, deciding to put all or most of your investment portfolio into the stock market is far more important than which individual stocks or which individual stock mutual funds you decide to use. Stock funds, as I will try to convince you in the next chapter, are an excellent vehicle for investing in the stock market. But the true secret of investment success is contained in this one notion: Put as much of your portfolio into the stock market as possible.

2

Mutual Benefits: Reasons for Favoring Stock Mutual Funds

Investing heavily in the stock market is the key to your investment success. So why use mutual funds? Why not buy individual stocks? You get some major benefits if you stick with stock funds:

- Stock mutual funds provide professional investment management, thereby saving you the need to try to pick individual stocks.
- Funds offer instant diversification, thus minimizing the risk that your portfolio will be severely hurt because one or two stocks turn sour. A mutual fund is, in essence, a company whose assets are the securities owned by the fund. Unless all of the stocks owned by the fund become worthless, there is no way that your stock fund shares can lose all of their value.
- Funds eliminate the accounting nightmare that can arise from trying to keep tabs on dividends and capital gains for dozens of different stocks. Stock funds gather together all

these various gains and pay them out to shareholders, normally at the end of December. Fund companies allow shareholders to automatically reinvest these gains in additional fund shares. You should use this service.

- Stock funds provide an inexpensive way of tapping into the stock market. The annual fees charged by stock funds typically range from 20 cents to $2 for every $100 invested. Investors are not sent a bill for these amounts. Instead, such expenses are gradually deducted throughout the year from a fund's share price.

- Mutual funds are within the reach of the most cash-strapped investors. While a few funds demand minimum initial investments of $50,000 or $100,000, most funds expect initial investments of between $1,000 and $3,000. Some funds—including some of the best—can be bought for $500 or less. Mutual funds, first introduced in the United States almost 70 years ago, were designed as a way for the small investor to get professional money management. But these days it is not just small investors who are buying mutual funds. Wealthy individuals and large institutional investors such as pension funds and charitable endowments are becoming major investors in mutual funds.

- Fund companies make it easy to get hold of your money—maybe too easy, given the tendency to panic in the face of a market downdraft. Every day that the stock market is open, you can buy and sell fund shares, often just by picking up the telephone. Many mutual funds are part of fund families, which include a host of different mutual funds. Investors can usually switch among these funds by phoning in their investment instructions. All buy or sell orders received by 4:00 P.M. Eastern time are transacted at the share price as of the close of the markets that day.

- Identifying top-notch mutual funds is relatively easy. It is not that all funds have been marvelous performers or that the companies that manage and sell mutual funds are benevolent "sugar daddies" who care only about their shareholders' best interests. The fund industry has sold a fair number of lousy funds, many of which should never have been introduced in the first place. But if you are willing to do a few rudimentary checks and to follow a systematic plan, it is possible to avoid the fund industry's turkeys and, over the long run, to make decent money.

▪ As with individual stocks, you can find out the value of your mutual fund holdings at any time by looking up the share prices (or net asset values, as fund share prices are more formally known) in the mutual fund quotations page of your local newspaper's business section. To figure out exactly what your funds are worth, simply multiply the number of shares you own by the fund share price.

▪ Mutual fund financial statements are audited, so you need never have any doubts about your funds' published performance results. By contrast, money managers who handle private accounts for the big institutional investors and rich individuals are notorious for playing statistical games with their performance results to make the results look as good as possible.

▪ Mutual funds are heavily regulated by the Securities and Exchange Commission (SEC). That helps protect you against the sort of inadequate disclosure, unethical behavior, and fraud that occasionally occur on Wall Street. There is no way, for instance, that a fund manager can steal the securities owned by a fund; those securities are held by a separate custodian. There is also no way that a fund can be affected if the fund's investment adviser gets into financial difficulty or if there is poor performance at another mutual fund in the same fund family; every mutual fund is a separate company with its own pool of assets.

▪ There is a final reason to invest in stock mutual funds rather than individual stocks, and it overshadows all of the reasons stated above. If you are going to enjoy the superior returns that the stock market generates over the long haul, you should try to ensure that your stocks do at least as well as the stock market averages.

That is where mutual funds come in. A typical stock mutual fund might own anywhere from 30 to 300 stocks. As a result, while any of the fund's individual stocks might nosedive into bankruptcy, the stock fund will tend to perform roughly in line with the broad market averages. That may seem a mixed blessing the next time the market crashes. But if your aim is to get the long-term benefits of stock market investing, the fact that a fund performs in keeping with the market averages is actually a major advantage.

Greatness Comes to the Mutual Fund Industry

Like Malvolio in Shakespeare's *Twelfth Night* (or so he thought), the mutual fund industry wasn't born great and it didn't achieve greatness, it had greatness thrust upon it. The first mutual fund, Massachusetts Investors Trust, was launched in 1924. But for decades afterward, the fund industry remained a financial backwater, in large part because of the damage done by the 1929 stock market crash and the atrocious performance of many closed-end funds.

The regulation of mutual funds was codified and tightened with the passage of the Investment Company Act of 1940. But despite the much tighter government regulation, investors continued to scorn mutual funds.

Helped along by some colorful stock fund managers, the fund industry finally started garnering attention in the 1960s. Jack Dreyfus's Dreyfus Fund emerged as the industry's most renowned fund as a result of both good performance and clever advertising. Go-go fund managers such as Fred Alger, Fred Carr, Fred Mates, and Gerald Tsai also briefly caught the public's imagination. But the public's enthusiasm was snuffed out in the 1969–70 and 1973–74 stock market downdrafts.

In the mid-1970s, the fund industry began to recover, in part because of the introduction of money market funds, and especially money market funds that offered check-writing privileges. Then came the explosive growth of the 1980s, as the long bull market in stocks and bonds drove the fund industry's assets from less than $95 billion at the end of 1979 to almost $1 trillion a decade later. Over the same period, the number of funds jumped from 524 to 2,918. Mutual funds suddenly emerged as the investment vehicle of choice for the small investor. In one brief decade, greatness was thrust upon the mutual fund industry.

Mutual funds are growing more popular every day, as investors pick bond funds over CDs and choose stock funds instead of individual stocks. Total fund assets now stand at $1.6 trillion. The stock fund portion alone is close to $500 billion, up from $33 billion at the start of the 1980s. Popularity is often a danger signal when it comes to investing. When the crowd grows too thick, this is often a sign that the object of its fascination—whether a particular stock or a particular fund or a particular investment style—is due for a tumble. But mutual funds have withstood the test of time pretty well, and their popularity is well deserved. Funds have become the little guy's way of tapping into the securities markets. But simply dumping some bucks into a few mutual funds isn't enough. Instead, investors must adopt an intelligent and systematic approach to stock fund investing. That is what this book is all about.

Where We Go from Here

Unlike many other books on mutual funds, the focus of *Funding Your Future* isn't on how to find the next superstar mutual fund or how to time the market. Unfortunately, there are no magic formulas for achieving either of those goals.

Market timing—the attempt to move money in and out of the stock market so that you catch bull markets but gracefully sidestep market crashes—may be a wonderful idea, but successful practitioners are rare indeed. Market timing is actually a very risky strategy. If you are a long-term investor, the worst thing that can happen is for the stock market to roar ahead while your portfolio is sitting in cash. It is far better to remain fully invested in stocks at all times and simply grit your teeth through the inevitable ups and downs.

The search for the next superstar mutual fund manager is a constant obsession of many fund investors. Indeed, most investors spend far too much time trying to find the next superstar mutual fund and not nearly enough time thinking about how they should allocate their money between stocks, bonds, and other investments.

Anybody who owned Fidelity Magellan Fund during the 1980s would have earned dazzling returns; the fund soared 1,124% during the decade, far more than any other stock fund. But if Magellan started out as only 10% of your portfolio and the other 90% was in a money market fund, your investment results would have been thoroughly mediocre. During the decade, your portfolio would have returned just 250%, compared with a 404% gain for the Standard & Poor's 500 stock index, which is a stock market average comprised of 500 larger-company stocks.

Over the next decade, there will be one fund that will beat all others. Which fund will it be? If you knew the answer, you would no doubt put all your money into that fund and then sit back and enjoy the results. But the fact is that nobody knows. The Wall Street pundits don't know. Mutual fund managers don't know. *Wall Street Journal* reporters certainly don't know.

That's why this book takes a different approach. Helping you identify top funds is one goal of *Funding Your Future*. But it is by no means the most important goal. Instead, this book aims to get you to think less about individual funds and more about portfolios of funds. The reason: It is a rare fund that does well year after year. Most successful fund managers pursue a single investment style. When a fund's investment style is in vogue, it is likely to beat the market. But at other times, a fund's performance will probably match or lag behind the market averages.

Thus if you own a fistful of well-run funds that use a variety of different investment styles, your fund portfolio should post decent gains in most market environments, even while the returns of the portfolio's component funds may at any one time vary from dazzling to mediocre.

But won't the losing funds cancel out the good performance of the winning funds? Not at all. Over time, all parts of the stock market should post gains. But different parts will do well at different times. If you bet all your money on a single fund representing a single part of the stock market, you could end up owning a fund whose investment style is going through a protracted dry spell. Only with a well-diversified portfolio can you be assured of getting a piece of the stock market's rise, wherever it is occurring, thereby providing an escape route if you need to cash in a part of your portfolio on short notice.

By building a mutual fund portfolio, you should enjoy not only healthy returns but also a smoother ride. If you're a nervous investor, the trick is to focus on how your total fund portfolio is performing, rather than dwelling on the fate of individual funds. If you focus on your portfolio's performance, you are far less likely to become rattled by the stock market's inevitable gyrations, because your portfolio's performance should be significantly more tranquil than that of the portfolio's component parts.

To help you put together a winning portfolio of mutual funds, *Funding Your Future* is divided into six parts, each of which deals with a major aspect of fund investing. In this first part, I have sought to make the case for investing in the stock market and have tried to convince you of the merits of stock mutual funds.

Part II details the major stock fund investment styles that

exist and explains why you should include a smattering of all of them in your stock fund portfolio.

In Part III, we look at how to pick individual stock mutual funds, including the importance of factors such as past performance, fund sales charges, and annual fund expenses.

The fourth part of this book looks at four strategies that you can use in building a winning stock fund portfolio. The chapters explain how to combine index funds, closed-end funds, and funds run by top-flight stock pickers. The chapters are accompanied by a series of sample mutual fund portfolios.

Part V looks at the criteria you should use in picking bond and money market funds and offers four strategies for bond fund investors. It also discusses when you should start introducing bond funds into your portfolio.

Part VI, the book's final two chapters, deals with the mechanics of fund investing and discusses some of the investment pitfalls you should seek to avoid. At the end of the book is an appendix that lists 100 popular or highly regarded stock and bond mutual funds, as well as a glossary that defines some of the terms used in this book.

3

Tools of the Trade: Where to Find the Information You Need

If you like baseball statistics, you will love mutual funds. Just as the national pastime has become the preserve of numbers-lovers, so the mutual fund industry has attracted a slew of research firms that are devoted to slicing and dicing fund statistics with all the enthusiasm of a Cuisinart.

Some of the data on mutual funds are arcane and unnecessary. But there is much that is useful. Before you start seriously considering whether a particular stock fund belongs in your portfolio, you need answers to nine key questions:

- Does the fund charge a sales commission?
- What are the fund's annual expenses?
- Who is the fund manager, and how long has he or she held the position?
- How much buying and selling of stocks does the fund manager do?
- What is the fund's minimum initial investment?
- How much money does the fund manage?

○ What is the fund's investment style?
○ How has the fund performed over the past 3, 5, and 10 years?
○ How has the fund performed in each of the last 10 calendar years?

The following chapters explain the significance of each item. Don't despair: You don't have to gather all this information for all funds. Some funds can be quickly dismissed on the basis of one or two obvious failings—you can't meet the investment minimum, the fund charges a sales commission, has high annual expenses, doesn't pursue an investment strategy that fits in a diversified portfolio, and so on.

Diligent fund investors should be able to round up all nine pieces of information by using three key sources—a fund's prospectus, a fund's annual report, and one of a fund's telephone service representatives.

A fund's prospectus is the official sales document that fund groups send to prospective investors. From a fund's prospectus, you can find out a fund's annual expenses, its minimum initial investment, how much trading the fund manager does, and whether the fund charges a sales commission.

If you want to find out how much money a fund manages, you can calculate the number using the prospectus, but it takes some figuring out. You may find it easier to look in a fund's annual report, where the total value of the fund's portfolio (also known as the fund's net assets) is given at the bottom of the listing that shows the portfolio's stock-by-stock breakdown. The fund's annual report should also contain data on its annual expenses and how much trading it does.

In recent years, some fund companies have gotten better about providing information to shareholders. The fund may, for instance, send you literature that includes performance information, details about the fund's investment style, and some biographical information on the fund's manager.

If that's not the case, try calling a fund's telephone service representatives. A list of fund groups and their telephone numbers can be found in table 1 on pages 20–22. All the companies listed are low-load and no-load fund groups, which means their funds charge little or nothing in the way of fund sales commissions. (Sales commissions are often known as "loads" in mutual fund lingo.)

Table 1

FUND GROUPS THAT OFFER NO-LOAD AND LOW-LOAD MUTUAL FUNDS

Fund Group/Location	Telephone Number
AARP Investment Program/Boston, MA	617-330-5400/800-253-2277
Acorn/Chicago, IL	800-922-6769
Aetna Mutual Funds/Hartford, CT	800-367-7732
American Heritage Group/New York, NY	212-474-7308
Babson Fund Group/Kansas City, MO	816-471-5200/800-422-2766
Baron Asset Fund/New York, NY	212-759-7700/800-992-2766
Bartlett Mutual Funds/Cincinnati, OH	513-621-4612/800-800-4612
Benham Group/Mountain View, CA	415-965-4274/800-472-3389
Berger Group/Denver, CO	303-329-0200/800-333-1001
Berwyn Group/Berwyn, PA	215-640-4330/800-824-2249
Blanchard Group of Funds/New York, NY	212-779-7979/800-922-7771
Boston Company Group/Boston, MA	800-225-5267
Brandywine Fund/Greenville, DE	302-656-6200
Bull & Bear Group/New York, NY	212-363-1100/800-847-4200
CGM Group/Boston, MA	617-859-7714/800-345-4048
Century Shares Trust/Boston, MA	617-482-3060/800-321-1928
Clipper Fund/Beverly Hills, CA	310-247-3940/800-776-5033
Columbia Funds/Portland, OR	503-222-3606/800-547-1707
Dodge & Cox Group/San Francisco, CA	415-434-0311
Dreman Mutual Group/Jersey City, NJ	201-332-8228/800-533-1608
Dreyfus Corp./Uniondale, NY	718-895-1206/800-645-6561
Evergreen Funds/Purchase, NY	914-694-2020/800-235-0064
Fasciano Fund/Chicago, IL	312-444-6050/800-848-6050
Federated Funds/Pittsburgh, PA	412-288-1900/800-245-5000
Fidelity Investments/Boston, MA	800-544-8888
First Eagle Fund of America/New York, NY	212-943-9200/800-451-3623
Flex-Funds/Dublin, OH	614-766-7000/800-325-3539
Fontaine Trust/Towson, MD	410-825-7894/800-247-1550
Founders Funds/Denver, CO	303-394-4404/800-525-2440

Table 1, continued

Fund Group/Location	Telephone Number
GIT Investment Funds/Arlington, VA	703-528-6500/800-336-3063
Gabelli & Co./Rye, NY	800-422-3554
Gateway Group/Milford, OH	513-248-2700/800-354-6339
Gintel Group/Greenwich, CT	203-622-6400/800-243-5808
Gradison Mutual Funds/Cincinnati, OH	513-579-5700/800-869-5999
Greenspring Fund/Lutherville, MD	410-823-5353/800-366-3863
Harbor Funds/Toledo, OH	419-247-2477/800-422-1050
IAI Funds/Minneapolis, MN	612-376-2600/800-945-3863
Invesco Funds Group/Denver, CO	303-930-6300/800-525-8085
Janus Group/Denver, CO	800-525-8983
Kaufmann Fund/New York, NY	212-344-2661/800-237-0132
Kleinwort Benson Group/New York, NY	212-687-2515/800-233-9164
LMH Fund/Westport, CT	203-226-4768/800-847-6002
Lazard Funds/New York, NY	212-632-6000/800-228-0203
Lexington Management/Saddle Brook, NJ	800-526-0056
Lindner Group/St. Louis, MO	314-727-5305
Loomis Sayles Funds/Boston, MA	617-482-2450/800-633-3330
Mathers Fund/Bannockburn, IL	708-295-7400/800-962-3863
Meridian Fund/Larkspur, CA	415-461-6237/800-446-6662
Monetta Fund/Wheaton, IL	708-462-9800/800-666-3882
Montgomery Funds/San Francisco, CA	415-627-2400/800-428-1871
Mutual Series Fund/Short Hills, NJ	201-912-2100/800-448-3863
Neuberger & Berman Group/New York, NY	212-476-8800/800-877-9700
Nicholas Group/Milwaukee, WI	414-272-6133
Northeast Investors Group/Boston, MA	617-523-3588/800-225-6704
Oakmark Fund/Chicago, IL	800-476-9625
Oberweis Emerging Growth Fund/Aurora, IL	708-897-7100/800-323-6166
PIMCO Funds/Newport Beach, CA	800-927-4648
Pax World Fund/Portsmouth, NH	603-431-8022/800-767-1729
Pennsylvania Mutual Fund/New York, NY	212-355-7311/800-221-4268
Perritt Group/Chicago, IL	312-649-6940/800-338-1579
Portico Funds/Milwaukee, WI	414-287-3808/800-228-1024
Reich & Tang Group/New York, NY	212-476-5050/800-221-3079
Robertson Stephens/San Francisco, CA	415-781-9700/800-766-3863
Rushmore Group/Bethesda, MD	301-657-1500/800-343-3355
SAFECO Mutual Funds/Seattle, WA	206-545-5530/800-426-6730
Salomon Brothers Asset Mgmt./New York, NY	800-725-6666
Schafer Value Fund/New York, NY	212-644-1800/800-343-0481
Schwab Funds/San Francisco, CA	800-526-8600
Scudder Funds/Boston, MA	617-439-4640/800-225-2470
Selected Funds/Chicago, IL	800-426-6562
Sit "New Beginning" Group/Minneapolis, MN	612-334-5888/800-332-5580
Sound Shore Fund/New York, NY	203-629-1980/800-551-1980
Southeastern Asset Management/Memphis, TN	901-761-2474/800-445-9469

Table 1, continued

Fund Group/Location	Telephone Number
SteinRoe Mutual Funds/Chicago, IL	312-368-7800/800-338-2550
Stratton Group/Plymouth Meeting, PA	215-941-0255/800-634-5726
Strong Funds/Milwaukee, WI	414-359-1400/800-368-1030
T. Rowe Price Associates/Baltimore, MD	410-547-2308/800-638-5660
Twentieth Century/Kansas City, MO	816-531-5575/800-345-2021
U.S. Boston Group/Lincoln, MA	617-259-1144/800-331-1244
USAA Group/San Antonio, TX	800-382-8722
United Services Funds/San Antonio, TX	210-308-1222/800-873-8637
Valley Forge Fund/Valley Forge, PA	215-688-6839/800-548-1942
Value Line Group/New York, NY	212-687-3965/800-223-0818
Vanguard Group/Valley Forge, PA	215-669-1000/800-662-7447
WPG Mutual Funds/New York, NY	212-908-9582/800-223-3332
Warburg, Pincus Funds/New York, NY	212-878-0600/800-888-6878
Wasatch Advisors Funds/Salt Lake City, UT	801-533-0777/800-345-7460
Yacktman Fund/Chicago, IL	312-201-1200/800-525-8258

Source: Morningstar, Inc.

Many telephone service reps are well briefed about their fund group's mutual funds and may be able to give you all nine pieces of information. But other reps are worse than useless. If you can't get the answers you seek, try calling back later. The next rep you get may be more helpful. If you have many questions, it helps to avoid calling between 3:00 P.M. and 4:00 P.M. Eastern time. That's when phone volume tends to be heaviest and phone reps are most harried.

Mutual Fund Directories

If you are trying to nail down information on a slew of different funds, you could end up spending hours leafing through prospectuses and annual reports and talking to phone reps. Fortunately, there is a simpler way: visit your local library or bookstore to get hold of one of the directories of mutual fund statistics.

Because fund directories tend to be fairly expensive, your first stop should probably be your library. If you can get hold of it, the best publication on mutual funds is undoubtedly *Morningstar Mutual Funds*, published out of Chicago by Morningstar, Inc. Every two weeks, Morningstar puts out a newsletter which typically covers around 130 stock or bond funds. In all, the firm publishes a regular roster of 10 biweekly newsletters, so that in the course of a 20-week period *Morningstar* covers every mutual fund of any consequence. A full year's subscription costs $395, so only those with a substantial portfolio should consider subscribing. *Morningstar* also offers a three-month trial subscription for $55.

Morningstar Mutual Funds can provide a host of useful information. A single page is devoted to each fund, giving detailed statistical information plus some pointed commentary. Each fund is rated on a five-star scoring system, which can be useful in selecting a fund, although it shouldn't be taken as gospel. The scoring system's major flaw is that a fund can continue to get a four- or five-star rating even when the fund manager responsible for the fund's stellar record has since retired or quit. Morningstar also puts out other publications. Of particular interest is Morningstar's two-volume *Mutual Fund Sourcebook*, which is published annually and provides in-depth statistical information on virtually all stock and bond funds. Again, the books are fairly expensive; the pair costs $225.

If you can't find either *Morningstar Mutual Funds* or Morningstar's *Mutual Fund Sourcebook*, there are alternatives that may be available at your library. If you have to buy them, none is especially cheap.

Five years of year-by-year performance data and information on expenses, sales charges, and fund telephone numbers can be found in books such as *The Mutual Fund Encyclopedia*, by Gerald Perritt (Dearborn Financial Publishing, Inc., Chicago, $35.95), *Standard & Poor's/Lipper Mutual Fund Profiles* (Standard & Poor's Corp., New York, published four times a year, $139 annual subscription or $51 for single copies), and *The Individual Investor's Guide to No-Load Mutual*

Funds, put out by Chicago's American Association of Individual Investors (International Publishing Corp., Chicago, $24.95).

For 10 years of annual returns plus other statistical data, see *The Handbook for No-Load Fund Investors*, by Sheldon Jacobs (The No-Load Fund Investor, Inc., Irvington, NY, $49), *IBC/Donoghue's Mutual Funds Almanac* (IBC/Donoghue, Inc., Ashland, MA, $39.95), and *CDA/Wiesenberger Mutual Funds Panorama* (CDA/Wiesenberger, Rockville, MD, $95). Of all the sources mentioned above, the best value for the money is probably Sheldon Jacobs's *Handbook for No-Load Fund Investors*.

An extensive list of funds is available from the Investment Company Institute, the trade group for the mutual fund industry. The institute publishes an annual directory, which includes fund telephone numbers, addresses, how much money a fund manages, fund investment minimums, and what sort of sales commission, if any, is charged by each fund. For a copy of the directory, send $5 to Directory of Mutual Funds, Investment Company Institute, 1600 M Street, NW, Suite 600, Washington, D.C. 20036.

Another good source is the Mutual Fund Education Alliance. The alliance's *Investor's Guide to Low-Cost Mutual Funds* can be purchased by sending $5 to Mutual Fund Education Alliance, 1900 Erie Street, Suite 120, Kansas City, MO 64116. The alliance's guide covers fewer funds than the Investment Company Institute's directory, but it does provide some information on performance and annual fund expenses.

Newsletters, Newspapers, and Magazines

Newspapers and magazines can provide a wealth of information for a modest price. *Forbes* magazine's annual mutual fund survey, published every year in late August, includes telephone numbers and full addresses for virtually all fund groups. *Barron's* quarterly mutual fund survey also provides a host of information, including phone numbers and information on fund performance, sales commissions, and the name and tenure of each fund's manager. The *Barron's* survey typically appears in late January, late April, late July, and late October.

Regular coverage of mutual funds is provided by many business publications, including *Barron's, Financial World, Forbes, Fortune, Investor's Business Daily, Kiplinger's Personal Finance, Money, Smart Money,* and the *Wall Street Journal.* I wouldn't suggest subscribing to these publications simply to read their stories on mutual funds. Nonetheless, one of the best ways to learn about mutual funds and to get comfortable with the subject is to read articles about mutual funds whenever you see them. This book aims to tell you all you need to know to start a successful mutual fund investment program. But to gain confidence as a fund investor, the passage of time, wide reading, and investing itself are probably more important. If you read widely, you will quickly start to see the same funds mentioned again and again; you will soon realize that identifying good mutual funds isn't quite the overwhelming task that it might seem initially.

There are dozens of newsletters devoted to mutual funds. Newsletters can be useful sources of performance information and news about mutual funds, particularly items such as fund manager changes and the introduction of new funds. But that is not the main goal of most fund newsletters. Most letters advocate either market timing or buying funds whose shares are showing some upward price momentum. I find neither strategy particularly convincing. Very few newsletters seem to base their buy and sell advice on an in-depth, fundamental analysis of individual mutual funds. And most aren't worth the $100 to $200 annual subscription fees that they charge.

A few newsletters, such as *Fidelity Insight* (Wellesley, MA), *No-Load Fund Investor* (Irvington, NY), *No-Load Fund Analyst* (San Francisco), *Mutual Fund Letter* (Chicago), Morningstar's

The 5-Star Investor (Chicago), *United Mutual Fund Selector* (Wellesley Hills, MA), and *Vanguard Adviser* (Brooklyn, NY), seem to provide prudent advice. If you are tempted to subscribe to any newsletter, first ask the newsletter to send you a few back copies. That way, you can get a better sense of what you will be paying for before you send off a check.

(Some of the publications listed above—such as *No-Load Fund Analyst, Morningstar Mutual Funds*, Gerald Perritt's *Mutual Fund Encyclopedia*, and *Standard & Poor's/Lipper Mutual Fund Profiles*—are put out by folks who also helped me to put together this book, either by providing me with data or by reading the manuscript. I don't see this as a glaring conflict of interest. After all, I mention their publications for the same reason I sought their help with the book—because I respect the quality of their work.)

Distributions? What Distributions?

Before taking a look at stock fund investment styles and how to pick individual funds, we must examine one of the more puzzling aspects of mutual fund investing: how performance is calculated.

I remember receiving a call from a *Wall Street Journal* reader about a story of mine that was accompanied by a table listing a group of top-performing funds, including Twentieth Century Select Investors. The caller wondered whether the list was intended to be a list of bad funds. His reasoning was that he owned Twentieth Century Select and the fund's share price at the time was no higher than when he had bought the fund four years earlier. In reality, the fund had beaten the Standard & Poor's 500 stock index in three of those four years. What, I asked, about all the income and capital gains distributions that the caller had received over the past four years and presumably reinvested in additional fund shares? He had no idea what I was talking about.

What are these income and capital gains distributions?

Every year funds are required by law to pay out to share-holders virtually all the dividend and interest income and all the capital gains that they earned during the year. By passing on these gains to shareholders, funds avoid paying taxes. The tax tab is instead picked up by the shareholders themselves.

Bond and money funds typically make these distributions every month. Stock funds, on the other hand, usually make no more than two distributions each year, and many stock funds content themselves with just a single distribution, paid out in December. If you look at the mutual fund quotation table in your newspaper toward the end of December, you will often see a slew of funds that suddenly drop in share price. These drops occur not because of stock market losses but because the funds are going ex-dividend, by paying out all the dividends, interest, and capital gains that they re-ceived during the course of the prior 12 months.

Any interest received from holding bonds and any divi-dends received from owning stocks are included in the in-come distributions. Any profits made from buying securities and then reselling them at higher prices are included in the capital gains distributions, unless the fund has sufficient losing trades to offset these winning trades. Some fund share-holders take these distributions in cash, but most reinvest them back into the fund, by purchasing additional fund shares. Even if you reinvest your income and capital gains distributions, you still have to pay taxes on the amounts involved.

Shocking News: Investors Make Money Despite Falling Fund Share Price

Some funds, which take their profits quickly, pay out virtu-ally all their capital gains each year. As a result, the fund's share price won't tend to rise over time, even though the fund may be making oodles of money for its shareholders.

Take CGM Capital Development Fund, one of the fund industry's top performers through the 1980s. It finished 1990 with its share price at $18.55, which is $1.95 below its share price 10 years earlier.

Had investors lost money in the fund? Not at all. Fund shareholders earned 412.2% over that 10-year period. Their increased wealth wasn't obvious from the fund's share price. Instead, the gains were reflected in the large capital gains distributions that the fund had paid out over the 10-year period, which many fund shareholders would have used to purchase additional fund shares.

How does this work? Imagine two funds that started out with $10 share prices. Both funds return 33.1% over the next three years, at a rate of 10% a year. The three-year, 33.1% return is more than triple the annual 10% return because of the effect of compounding. One fund doesn't pay out any capital gains or income distributions. (In reality, this is highly unlikely to happen, because of IRS rules that compel funds to pay out virtually all dividends and capital gains each year.) Instead, over three years, the fund's share price—or net asset value—simply rises from $10 to $13.31.

The other fund pays out all of the capital gains and income that it earns. During each year, the fund's share price would rise, only to drop at year-end when the fund went ex-dividend and paid out all its dividends and capital gains. After three years, the fund's share price finishes up at $10, just where it started. But along the way, because of the distributions, a shareholder who was reinvesting all dividends and capital gains would have seen his number of shares rise from 1 to 1.331. Leaving aside the issue of taxes, shareholders in both funds would have done equally well—even though, in the second instance, the fund's share price ended up exactly where it began.

☐PART II☐
DECIPHERING STOCK FUND INVESTMENT STYLES

4

Multiple Choices: Getting a Handle on the Five Fund Investment Styles

Many mutual fund investors are impulse buyers. They read rave reviews for a particular stock fund, so they buy it. Then they hear about another potential superstar, so they invest in that fund as well. Before long, these investors own dozens of different funds, which together generate mediocre returns and massive accounting headaches. Their mistake: These investors never decided what types of stock funds they ought to own and in what sorts of quantities.

Every fund has a distinctive investment style. Some buy only U.S. stocks, others venture abroad. Some look for "growth" companies with rapidly increasing earnings, while others buy "value" stocks that are cheap relative to corporate assets or current earnings. Some buy the stocks of larger companies, and others dabble in only the very smallest stocks. In all, most stock funds can be slotted into one of five categories: small-company value, small-company growth, large-company value, large-company growth, and international.

These investment styles go in and out of favor. Take value funds that invest in larger U.S. companies. Through much of the 1980s, these were the fund industry's superstars. Stock funds such as John Neff's Windsor Fund, Mario Gabelli's Gabelli Asset Fund, and Michael Price's Mutual Shares Fund notched up big gains, partly because the gentlemen who run these funds are good stock-pickers, but also because the stocks favored by value investors were in vogue.

The sizzling performance of these funds climaxed in 1988, when Windsor rose 28.7%, Mutual Shares climbed 30.7%, and Gabelli Asset jumped 31.1%. The average stock fund, meanwhile, gained just 14.4%.

But that, it turned out, was the end of the party. In 1989, value investing went out of favor and to the fore came growth stock-pickers, such as the fund managers at Janus Group of Mutual Funds in Denver and the folks at Twentieth Century Investors in Kansas City, Missouri. Why such changes occur is difficult to say. In part, it is simply that one investment style grows excessively popular while another is excessively neglected, so that a correction is due. In this instance, the catalyst for the correction may have been a slowing of the takeover frenzy that during the 1980s had led to bidding wars for poorly run companies that were cheap based on assets or earnings or cash flow. These were just the sorts of companies favored by value investors.

After an initial surge in 1989, growth investors continued to prosper through 1990 and 1991, because many of the companies they favored generated earnings gains despite the recession. Growth funds such as Berger 100 Fund, Janus Twenty Fund, and Twentieth Century Ultra Investors were heralded as the fund industry's new superstars.

But in early 1992, as the economy struggled out of recession, growth funds faltered and value funds returned to the fore. Value funds were big holders of economically sensitive cyclical companies, such as the auto makers, the chemical producers, and the paper companies. As investors anticipated an end to the recession, they flocked to these stocks, helping to revive the performance of value funds. After a three-year drought, Gabelli Asset Fund, Mutual Shares Fund, and Windsor Fund were once again beating the market.

Growth Versus Value

For many investors, the most confusing aspect of fund investing is the distinction between growth funds and value funds. Knowing the difference is crucial in putting together a diversified portfolio of mutual funds.

Among value managers, there are four stock-picking strategies that are especially popular. First, some value investors look for stocks that are undervalued based on corporate assets. Such assets might include real estate that the company owns but isn't using for any corporate purpose; just by selling the land, the company can realize a one-time gain. Often a management change may be the spark that causes the selling of underutilized assets. Sometimes the catalyst is a corporate raider, who has either taken over the company or is threatening to do so unless the company sells assets to "maximize shareholder value."

Second, value investors like stocks that are cheap compared to current earnings. One of the most widely used yardsticks of a stock's value is its price-to-earnings multiple, known in Wall Street shorthand as a company's P/E. A P/E ratio tells you what the relationship is between a company's stock price and its earnings during the most recent year. Thus, if a company earned $3 a share over the past year and its stock was trading at $45, it would have a P/E ratio of 15, which is arrived at by dividing the $45 stock price by the $3 in earnings.

Historically, stocks have traded at around 14 times the

earnings that companies have generated over the prior 12 months. But during bear markets, average P/E ratios have fallen as low as 6, and during bull markets they have climbed above 20. Value investors typically gravitate toward stocks with below-average P/Es. If stocks on average are trading at, say, 17 times earnings, value investors will typically be buying stocks with P/Es that are 16 and below.

Third, some value players put a lot of weight on cash flow. Cash flow has numerous definitions, but in essence it is another way of looking at earnings. Cash flow measures try to give a better sense of how much cash a company is generating. They do that by stripping away the accounting conventions that sometimes make earnings seem unnecessarily depressed.

Finally, some value managers like to buy stocks with above-average dividend yields. A stock's dividend yield is calculated by taking the cash dividends per share paid out over the past year by a company and then dividing that figure by the company's current stock price. Thus a stock that kicks off an annual dividend of 40 cents and trades at $10 would have a dividend yield of 4%.

By contrast, growth-stock investors pay scant attention to dividends or corporate assets. Oftentimes growth investors will buy stocks that trade at lofty P/E ratios and that pay little or nothing in the way of dividends. Sometimes they will buy companies that are adding new stores, offices, or equipment so quickly that they are forced to borrow money because they aren't generating enough cash to finance their own growth.

Why are growth-stock pickers willing to buy such stocks? Because the stocks have potentially fabulous future earnings. Growth funds are frequently large holders of fast-growing health care and technology companies, both of which typically command above-average P/E ratios. Changes in earnings are the biggest factor in driving stock prices. As a result, a successful growth company can see its stock post healthy price gains year in and year out.

Putting Funds in Their Place

How should you go about distinguishing growth funds from value funds? Here are a few signposts to look for. None are necessarily conclusive, but together they may help you slot a fund into the growth category or the value category:

▪ Look at recent fund performance. According to Lipper Analytical Services, the average stock mutual fund returned 14.4% in 1988, 24% in 1989, -6.3% in 1990, 35.6% in 1991, and 8.9% in 1992. Value funds generally did better than average in 1988 and 1992, but lagged during 1989, 1990, and 1991. Conversely, growth funds lagged behind the average in 1988 and 1992 but posted above-average returns in 1989, 1990, and 1991.

▪ Look at a fund's annual portfolio turnover, which reflects how much buying and selling a fund manager does. These figures can usually be found in a fund's prospectus or annual report. Growth funds typically do a lot of trading and have turnover of 100% and above, while value funds will generally have much lower turnover.

▪ Look at how a fund is classified. Companies that track mutual fund performance, like Lipper Analytical Services and Morningstar, Inc., divide funds into categories such as "growth" and "growth-and-income." But these categories merely reflect differing investment goals—whether a fund emphasizes current income or capital gains or some combination of the two. The categories are not intended to reflect the investment styles of the constituent funds. There is, for instance, no Lipper or Morningstar category that is called "value."

As a rule of thumb, value funds tend to be thrown into the

"equity-income" or "growth-and-income" categories, because value funds frequently buy stocks with higher dividend yields. Growth funds, meanwhile, will often be stuck into the "growth," "aggressive growth," or "capital appreciation" categories. But there are no guarantees. Within any one category you are likely to find funds that pursue both investment styles.

▪ Look at a fund's dividend yield, which you can get from a fund's telephone service representatives. Funds with dividend yields of 3% and above will tend to be value funds. Those with low or no dividend payout will typically be growth-stock funds.

Medium-sized and smaller fund companies often have a house investment style, thus making it easier to figure out how the company's funds are run. Founders Funds, Invesco Funds Group, Janus Group of Mutual Funds, and Twentieth Century Investors all use a growth-stock style. Value investing, meanwhile, predominates at Babson Fund Group, Gabelli & Co., Lindner Group, and Neuberger & Berman Group. (One exception: Gabelli Growth Fund uses a growth-stock style, unlike the rest of the Gabelli funds.)

Some funds don't seem to fall cleanly into either the growth camp or the value camp. Conservative growth funds, such as Evergreen Fund or Nicholas Fund, look for growth stocks, but they generally aren't willing to buy stocks with high P/E ratios. As a result, I tend to lump conservative growth funds into the value camp, because both types of funds typically own stocks with P/Es that are below the market average. For the growth camp, I reserve funds like the earnings momentum funds, which look for companies with rapid and sometimes accelerating earnings growth, and emerging growth funds, which buy companies that have a lot of promise for future profitability but which may have no current earnings.

If you can't figure out how a fund is managed, try calling

the fund group involved. You may also find it helpful to look at the appendix at the end of this book. The appendix includes a list of stock funds categorized by their investment style.

A lot of time is spent debating the relative merits of growth and value investing. Because they favor stocks that are cheaper relative to earnings and dividends, value funds tend to be less volatile than growth funds and they often perform better during market crashes. As a result, value funds are frequently favored by retirees and more conservative investors. The share price of a growth fund, on the other hand, can bounce around fairly sharply. Over time, however, growth funds can post spectacular gains, so investment advisers frequently steer younger investors toward these funds.

Whatever your age, it is advisable to have money in both growth funds and value funds so that your portfolio's performance won't be wholly dependent on just one investment style. It is tough to sit tight if your value fund is eking out modest gains while your neighbor's growth fund is soaring. In all likelihood, your frustration will overwhelm you, and you will dump your value fund and buy a growth fund—just at the point when value funds come back into favor.

A Question of Size

Just as it is possible to slot most funds into the value camp or the growth camp, so it is possible to sort funds based on the size of the companies they buy. Funds can be divided roughly into two camps: those that buy shares in companies with stock market values of $1 billion and up and those that stick with smaller stocks. A company's stock market value is calculated by multiplying its share price by the number of shares the company has outstanding.

From 1975 to 1983, small-company stock funds led the market while large-company stock funds lagged. But then the cycle turned. From mid-1983 through late 1990, large-company stock funds soared and small-stock funds sagged. As of this writing, it seems that small-stock funds are once again taking the lead.

For investors, it makes sense to own both small-stock funds and large-company stock funds, just as it is prudent to own some funds run by growth stock-pickers and some managed by value investors. Because investment styles go in and out of favor, and nobody can know for sure when those style switches might occur or how long the cycles might run, the intelligent investor should make sure he is exposed to all these market segments.

If a fund invests primarily in smaller-company stocks, that is usually made clear in the fund's prospectus or in any other literature the fund might send you. But even without ordering a prospectus, it is relatively easy to find out whether a fund invests in small-company stocks. Lipper Analytical Services and Morningstar, for instance, have a special category devoted to small-company stock funds. Both firms put out their own publications. In addition, *Barron's*, *Business Week*, and *Money* include Lipper or Morningstar fund classifications in their regular surveys of mutual fund performance.

Not all funds that invest in small-company stocks are classified that way by Lipper or Morningstar. Brandywine Fund and Strong Common Stock Fund, for instance, typically buy stocks with stock market values below $1 billion. By prospectus, however, both funds aren't limited to smaller stocks. As a result, Lipper and Morningstar classify these funds as growth funds, not small-company funds.

There is some debate about what actually constitutes "small." Many small-stock funds, like Baron Asset Fund, Monetta Fund, and Nicholas II, buy companies with average stock market values of around $500 million. But a handful of funds, such as GIT Equity Trust-Special Growth, T. Rowe Price Small-Cap Value Fund, Shadow Stock Fund, and Vanguard Small Capitalization Stock Fund, stick mostly with the smallest of the small stocks, those with market values of

$200 million and below. These tiny stocks have, over long periods of time, generated superior returns compared with the rest of the stock market; this is the so-called small-firm effect. Chicago's Ibbotson Associates calculates that these tiny stocks have returned around 9 percentage points a year more than inflation since 1926, compared with 7 percentage points a year above inflation for the Standard & Poor's 500 stock index.

Venturing Abroad

There is a third way that investors should diversify—by investing overseas. U.S. stocks now account for only about a third of world stock market value. That doesn't mean that you should invest two-thirds of your portfolio abroad. But for aggressive investors, a good case can be made for putting as much as 40% of your fund assets into foreign stock funds.

Foreign economies seem likely to grow faster than the U.S. economy in the decades ahead. And if U.S. inflation persists in running ahead of the inflation rate in countries like Japan and Germany, investors can expect that over the long term the dollar will continue slipping in the foreign exchange market, which in turn will make foreign stocks more valuable for U.S. investors. Exchange rate fluctuations make foreign stocks doubly volatile. Not only do foreign stocks bounce up and down in price, but the value of those stocks in U.S. dollars fluctuate along with exchange rate movements.

Through the 1980s, international stock funds like T. Rowe Price International Stock Fund and Scudder International Fund outstripped U.S. stock market yardsticks like the Standard & Poor's 500 stock index and the Dow Jones Industrial Average. But international funds offer more than just the prospect of better performance. If you own U.S. stock funds, adding an international fund will help dampen the gyrations in your portfolio's value. International stock funds have had a tendency to perform well when domestic stock funds are doing poorly, and vice versa. Indeed, some investment advisers reckon that the best way to diversify a stock fund portfolio is to keep a hefty chunk invested in foreign stocks.

International stock funds posted fat gains from 1985 to 1987. According to Morningstar, these funds even gained more than 7% in 1987, the year the stock market crashed and most U.S. stock funds barely made any money at all. But anybody who took 1987's strong performance as a reason to invest exclusively in international funds would have been sorely disappointed. From 1989 to 1992, international funds lagged behind domestic funds.

The moral of the story? Just as it is advisable to own both growth and value funds and to buy both small-company and large-company funds, so it makes sense to invest in both U.S. and foreign stock funds. How many funds does this mean you should buy? To tap into the various investment styles, you should purchase at least five stock funds: a small-company growth fund, a large-company growth fund, a small-company value fund, a large-company value fund, and an international fund.

5

Mixing It Up: Why You Should Own Different Funds

Here's the sad truth: Owning a mutual fund portfolio can be thoroughly irksome. The more mutual funds you own, the more mutual fund statements you have to keep track of. There's no getting around it. This is an extremely tedious task.

Is it worth the hassle? I think so. By buying different sorts of stock funds, you should end up with a portfolio that generates greater returns but doesn't necessarily involve bigger day-to-day swings in the value of your portfolio.

To get superior returns, you need to venture into some of the better-performing segments of the mutual fund world, like small-company stock funds and international stock funds. But many investors shy away from these funds. The reason: They can't stand the gut-wrenching swings in share price. Instead, these investors stick only with more sedate funds that invest in large-company stocks.

Now imagine that you combine volatile foreign-stock funds and small-company stock funds with more staid funds that

buy large-company stocks. Because of the better performance of small-stock funds and foreign-stock funds, you
should get better returns than if you stuck only with large-
company stock funds. But here is the twist: This extra-long-
term return shouldn't be accompanied by a big increase in
the volatility of your portfolio. This is, in essence, the magic
of diversification.

How does it work? Because the stock market rises over
time, all your stock funds should eventually post decent
gains. But different types of stock funds tend to do well at
different times. Thus when one fund is heading into the tank,
another fund may be riding high. These price movements
will, to some extent, offset one another, so that your portfolio
will be more tranquil than if you owned any one fund on its
own.

Most investors fail to properly diversify their portfolios, so
they end up suffering through a lot more share-price gyrations than they really have to. But don't be misled. There is
a limit to what diversification can achieve. With a portfolio
that is entirely invested in stock mutual funds, you are still
going to get some pretty wild price swings, even if you are
properly diversified.

A Brief (and Occasionally Painful) History

Here is how diversification might work in practice. Consider a portfolio that was put together by investing in five
stock funds, each representing one of the five investment
styles. The funds are Vanguard/Morgan Growth Fund (large-
company growth), Neuberger & Berman Guardian Fund
(large-company value), Evergreen Fund (small-company
value), Vanguard Explorer Fund (small-company growth),
and Kleinwort Benson International Equity Fund (international). These aren't necessarily the mutual funds you would
want to buy today, nor do all of these funds rank as top
performers. But for the purpose of this exercise, these funds

have two distinct virtues. They have all been around since 1973, and they have all used the same investment advisory firm (though not necessarily the same individual portfolio manager) throughout the period.

Imagine that you had put equal amounts of money in each of the five funds at the beginning of January 1973. With any portfolio, you don't want to be overweighted in some funds and underweighted in others. To avoid this problem, the imaginary portfolio was rebalanced annually, so that you started each year with the same amount invested in each fund. (In practice, you probably would want to invest less in the small-company stock funds and more in the large-company funds and the international fund, but we will leave the question of portfolio weightings until Part IV.) Table 2 (p. 44) shows how your portfolio, and the constituent funds, would have performed.

Take a single glance at the table and one event immediately jumps out at you: the 1973–74 market crash, the worst period for the stock market since the Great Depression. The Standard & Poor's 500 stock index tumbled 37% in two years as oil prices skyrocketed, inflation took off, and the U.S. economy sunk into a recession.

Table 2 could have been started at 1975, simply ignoring the 1973–74 crash. But once in a while—maybe once in everybody's investing lifetime—the market will get hit by a crash like that of 1973–74, so it is helpful to know just how bad things can get. The unfortunate lesson: If the stock market really gets creamed, so will you. It doesn't matter how well diversified your stock fund portfolio is. The fact is that diversification only works because different types of stock funds generally do well at different times. It doesn't help when everything bombs out all at once.

In other recent market crashes, a diversified portfolio would have fared much better. In 1987, U.S. stock funds got hit hard, but international stock funds provided some offsetting gains. In 1977, large-company stock funds had a

Table 2

MIXED BLESSINGS: HOW ONE STOCK FUND PORTFOLIO WOULD HAVE FARED

	Vanguard Morgan Growth (Large-company growth)	Neuberger & Berman Guardian (Large-company value)	Evergreen Fund (Small-company value)	Vanguard Explorer Fund (Small-company growth)	Kleinw't Benson Int'l (Int'l)	Five-fund average	S&P 500
1973	−19.1%	−12.4%	−26.2%	−26.1%	−3.2%	−17.4%	−14.7%
1974	−32.3	−15.0	−21.4	−35.1	−12.2	−23.2	−26.5
1975	43.1	40.7	60.1	22.8	32.4	39.8	37.2
1976	19.1	36.1	48.9	16.8	1.5	24.5	23.9
1977	7.5	−1.2	25.3	28.1	5.8	13.1	−7.1
1978	19.3	8.9	38.0	20.6	25.6	22.5	6.6
1979	18.9	37.9	46.9	33.8	15.6	30.6	18.6
1980	34.7	30.2	48.1	55.4	49.1	43.5	32.5
1981	−4.8	−4.7	−1.6	1.9	−14.6	−4.8	−4.9
1982	27.7	28.7	19.7	41.4	−15.9	20.3	21.6
1983	28.4	25.3	30.1	20.5	33.0	27.4	22.6
1984	−6.1	7.4	0.0	−19.5	−14.4	−6.5	6.3
1985	30.3	25.3	35.4	22.4	54.1	33.5	31.7
1986	7.8	11.9	13.0	−8.4	52.6	15.4	18.7
1987	5.0	−1.0	−3.0	−6.9	9.3	0.7	5.3
1988	22.3	28.1	23.0	25.9	21.0	24.1	16.6
1989	22.7	21.5	15.0	9.4	23.0	18.3	31.6
1990	−1.5	−4.7	−11.7	−10.8	−14.8	−8.7	−3.1
1991	29.3	34.3	40.1	55.9	11.8	34.3	30.4
1992	9.5	19.0	8.7	13.0	−3.4	9.4	7.6
1973–1992*	11.4%	14.5%	16.9%	10.2%	10.6%	13.2%	11.3%
1975–1992*	16.6%	18.1%	22.5%	16.0%	12.9%	17.7%	15.6%

*Annualized returns

Source: Lipper Analytical Services

rough time, but small-company stock funds posted dazzling results. By contrast, the 1973–74 market crash was a rare occurrence, a market collapse where all funds got hit hard, so that investors got no benefits from owning a diversified portfolio.

How bad was the 1973–74 crash? Not quite as bad as it might initially seem. For starters, the market had run up 78% over the prior six years. The 37% loss suffered during the crash would have been most fully felt by those unfortunate enough to have put all their money in at the market's peak. For investors who had followed a more prudent strategy of putting their money gradually into the stock market over time, the 1973–74 crash wouldn't have been nearly so devastating.

Nonetheless, our five-fund portfolio lost 17% in 1973 and another 23% in 1974, for a combined loss of 37%. (The 37% is less than the sum of the two annual losses because of the way compounding works.) But for those tenacious enough to hang on, the five-fund portfolio quickly recovered. Within two years, the portfolio had earned back all of the 37% loss, and then some. And despite the portfolio's overall loss during the 1973–74 crash, some benefits were gained from owning a diversified portfolio of stock mutual funds. International funds, often seen as one of the riskiest fund investments, proved their worth during this period. The international fund lost only 15% of its value during 1973 and 1974, thus helping to soften the blow suffered by the other funds.

While diversification didn't help much during the 1973–74 crash, it proved invaluable in the 18 years that followed. In the period of 1975–92, the large-company value fund and the small-company growth fund each had four years when they suffered a loss, while the large-company growth fund and the small-company value fund both got hit with three losing years. The international fund had a particularly tough time. During four of its five losing years, it got pounded for losses of 14% and more.

If you had owned any one of the five funds on its own, you would have had a rough ride. But as part of a diversified portfolio, the ups and downs of the various funds became far less significant. Because each fund's losses tended to happen at different times, the five-fund portfolio had only three down years during the 18 years between 1975 and 1992, the worst of which was an 8.7% loss in 1990. For contrast, look at what happened to the S&P 500 over the same period. Like our five-fund portfolio, the S&P 500 also suffered three losing years. Its worst down year was only marginally less painful than that suffered by the five-fund portfolio. Thus the five-fund portfolio seems about as risky as the S&P 500. And what about returns? It is no contest. The five-fund portfolio beat the S&P 500 by a comfortable margin.

Five Funds, Four Benefits

By owning a diversified portfolio of five funds, you should get four key benefits. First, you should get better returns than those posted by the S&P 500. That is a less surprising result than you might think. Foreign stocks and small-company stocks are likely to enjoy more rapid earnings growth than the S&P 500 companies, so over long time periods they should post superior stock market gains. By including small-company stocks and international stocks in your portfolio, you should get better returns over the long haul.

Second, investment styles go in and out of favor, so that by ensuring that you are invested in all market sectors, you end up with a portfolio that is more tranquil than its component funds. That can make it a little easier to bear the daily ups and downs of the stock market—provided you can focus on the performance of your portfolio rather than the wild swings suffered by individual funds.

But as the 1973–74 bear market shows, there is a limit to how much volatility you can avoid by diversifying among different types of stock funds. Unfortunately, the only surefire way to dampen fluctuations in your portfolio's value is to own low-returning but stable investments like money market funds and bond funds. But only the most skittish investors should start buying money market funds and bond funds simply to make their portfolios more tranquil.

Diversification has a third advantage: You boost the likelihood that at least some portion of your portfolio will be doing well at any given time. That can be a big plus should you have to cash in a part of your stock fund portfolio at short notice. If necessary, you can sell those funds that are riding high, thereby avoiding the need to sell a portion of your portfolio that is currently in a slump.

There is a fourth major benefit that comes from picking funds based on their investment styles. By doing so, you are far less likely to end up putting an excessive amount of money into a hot stock market sector just before the sector nosedives. One of the most common investment errors is to buy a group of stock funds merely because they were among the top performers for the past three years or the past five years. If you do that, you are likely to end up owning a fistful of funds that all do essentially the same thing—after all, that is the reason they all ended up at the top of the performance charts at the same time.

If you pick funds based on their different styles, you will probably end up with one or two funds that have done well over the past few years. You may also, however, end up buying funds that have had a so-so record compared to the broad market averages but a great record compared to funds that use a similar investment style. At the start of 1991, for instance, anybody looking to buy a small-company stock fund had to choose from among some funds with absolutely miserable long-term performances. But if you completely dismissed these funds from consideration because of their lackluster long-term records, you would have missed the chance to reap big gains in 1991's small-stock bull market.

Mutual Antipathy

Some stock funds don't fit into the five categories listed above. In chapter 11, you will find out about a peculiar breed of mutual fund known as the index fund, which you might also want to own. Unlike the funds described above, index funds don't do any active stock-picking. Instead, they buy and hold the stocks that make up a particular market index, like the Standard & Poor's 500 stock index, in an effort to match the index's performance. By buying index funds, you can guarantee that you will do about as well as the market averages. Because of that virtue, owning a mix of index funds can help complement a portfolio of actively managed stock funds, whose returns are far less predictable.

But there are other funds that, however worthy on their own merits, shouldn't be a part of your mutual fund portfolio. For instance, of the two main types of funds that buy foreign stocks—international funds and global funds—only international funds invest exclusively abroad. Global funds buy both U.S. and foreign stocks. If you are seeking foreign stock exposure as part of a diversified fund portfolio, avoid global funds because you won't be getting a pure foreign play.

Similarly, there are funds, such as balanced funds and asset allocation funds, that own a mixture of stocks and bonds. Some of these funds shift between the two types of securities depending on market conditions, while others maintain a fixed allocation between stocks and bonds. Global funds, asset allocation funds, and balanced funds appeal to those looking for a single fund that will somehow meet all of their investment needs. The problem is that these funds often have such broad investment charters that it is difficult to know exactly what you are getting. Asset allocation and balanced funds, in particular, tend to be postured too conservatively for the long-term investor, because of their large holdings of bonds.

A growing number of funds invest in the stocks of a single industry sector, such as biotechnology or energy or gold. These funds appeal to people looking for that knockout fund that will propel them to untold riches. There have been a few funds that have consistently beaten the market for years on end, for various reasons: because they were invested in the right sector, because they were skillfully run by an agile stock-picker, or because they were lucky. But these funds are rare indeed, and their winning streaks are apparent only in hindsight.

Betting the bank on one fund, particularly a risky fund like a sector fund, certainly has the potential to be hugely rewarding. But this strategy is far more likely to generate roller-coaster returns and lots of anxiety. That is why you are better advised to assemble a portfolio of funds that will—taken together—produce healthy returns in a variety of market environments. After all, if you are going to take the risk of investing in the stock market, the worst possible outcome is to not be decently rewarded for the risk that you take.

☐PART III☐
TRACKING DOWN STELLAR STOCK FUNDS

6

Many Happy Returns: Identifying Top-Performing Funds

Many investors think that tracking down a top-performing stock fund is the trickiest part of fund investing. In fact, it is a cinch. Fund groups aren't shy about advertising their successes. Magazines like *Forbes*, *Kiplinger's Personal Finance*, *Money*, and *Smart Money* are littered with ads from fund groups. So too are the business pages of major newspapers. Every fund group, it seems, has a fund that is ranked number 1 over some time period or other.

And then, of course, there are the endless lists. Publications like *Barron's*, *Business Week*, *Fortune*, *Forbes*, *Investor's Business Daily*, *Kiplinger's*, *Money*, and the *Wall Street Journal* frequently run tables of top-performing funds. Some of these publications even present comprehensive annual surveys of fund performance. Local libraries can be gold mines of information, in terms of both business magazines and the more specialized fund publications listed in chapter 3.

Some fund shareholders choose to make their lives easy

by keeping all their money with one of the large fund groups. Major firms like Fidelity Investments, T. Rowe Price Associates, and Vanguard Group each offer all or most of the different funds you need to put together a diversified fund portfolio. But oftentimes some of the best funds within each investment style are part of smaller fund groups that don't advertise heavily and get relatively little publicity. To help you find such funds, a list of some highly regarded funds can be found in the appendix. All the funds listed in the appendix charge little or nothing in the way of fund sales commissions.

By using these various sources, you should be able to put together a fairly long list of top-performing funds that you might want to include in your portfolio. Some of these funds will boast good three-year or five-year records; others may claim high returns for the past decade.

Step Number 1: Sorting Funds by Investment Style

Once you have put together a list of top-performing funds, the first step is to sort each of these star performers into one of five groups, depending on each fund's investment style, whether it be small-company value, small-company growth, large-company value, large-company growth, or international. After all, you are looking not just for one good fund, but for five funds representing each of the five investment styles. As mentioned in chapter 5, not all funds fit into these five categories, and those that don't should probably be ignored. Once you know what style a fund uses, you can compare its record to other funds using the same investment style.

Sometimes, as in the case of large-company value funds, you will have a fair number of good funds on your list. In other instances, such as with small-company value funds, you won't have much choice at all. As a rule of thumb, growth-stock managers lean toward smaller stocks, so there tend to be more small-company growth funds than small-company value funds. Conversely, value managers seem to have an overwhelming preference for bigger companies, so there are a decent number of large-company value funds to choose from.

Don't allow yourself to become overwhelmed in your search for top-performing funds. There is no need to scour the country for every last mutual fund, fearful that you might miss out on the next superstar. Discovering the next super-star fund (if it indeed exists) may be an enticing thought, but the goal here is somewhat more modest. At the very least, you are trying to avoid the turkeys of the mutual fund indus-try and in the process you will hopefully end up with funds that are above-average performers.

Remember, most funds—over time—perform reasonably well. Among diversified domestic stock funds, 89% would have tripled your money during the course of the 1980s and 60% would have quadrupled your money, according to data from Lipper Analytical Services. As long as you bypass the poorest performers and make the right allocation decisions in terms of being in stocks and owning the right types of stock funds, you will have a good chance of investment success.

When picking funds, compare the three-, five-, and ten-year records of each set of funds that use the same invest-ment style. A small-company value fund should be compared to other small-company value funds, and an international stock fund should be stacked up against other international stock funds.

Look particularly for funds with strong five-year records, though also consider funds that have performed well over three and ten years. Why not just focus on funds with good ten-year records? These funds, after all, would seem to be the ones that have truly proved their worth. The trouble is that many funds have been launched in recent years and if you restrict yourself to strong ten-year performers, you are likely to miss out on some well-managed funds. In addition, any fund with a strong ten-year record is likely to have attracted a lot of money from investors, and the fund may now be large and unwieldy. If you look for funds with good five-year records, you are more likely to find funds that are well-run but aren't yet too large.

Misstep Number 1: Comparing Apples and Oranges

When looking at fund track records, make sure that the performance numbers you are comparing cover the same period of time. I once got a letter from a reader who was curious about the disparity between three sets of performance numbers, those shown in the *Wall Street Journal*, those in the *New York Times*, and those in his fund's annual report. As it turned out, the reader had failed to notice that each of the three publications used a different time period. The *Journal*'s data were for the year through December 31, 1991, the *Times*' data concluded on December 26, and the fund's annual report used data through October 31.

Because of stock market fluctuations, it is meaningless to compare, say, the five years ended June 30 for one fund with the five years ended July 31 for another fund. Fidelity Magellan Fund, for instance, returned 2,004.2% over the ten years ended September 30, 1987. Move ahead just one month, so that you are looking at the ten years ended October 31, 1987, and Magellan's ten-year record drops to 1,542%, according to Lipper Analytical Services. The difference? In October 1987, the stock market crashed. Market crashes are, of course, rare occurrences, but the point remains the same: If you are going to compare the track records of two funds, make sure you are looking at the same time period.

There's an additional pitfall to look out for. Fund performance numbers can be expressed on either a cumulative or an annualized basis. For instance, if a fund doubles shareholders' money during a five-year period, its cumulative return would be 100% and its annualized return 14.9%. In other words, the fund returned an average 14.9% each year. The 100% cumulative return is more than five times the 14.9% annualized return because of the way compounding works. When comparing two sets of performance numbers, check to make sure that one set of numbers isn't expressed on an annualized basis and the other on a cumulative basis.

A fund group's phone reps should be able to give you mutual fund performance data. You could also consult one of the mutual fund directories or one of the magazine surveys of fund performance. Either way, the performance numbers you get will be so-called total return numbers. Total return performance numbers take into account both the movement of a fund's share price and the reinvestment of any capital gains and income distributions.

Falling Stars

For each of the five fund investment styles, it's pretty easy to identify the funds with the best records. So you should just buy these funds, right? Unfortunately not.

Often you will want to avoid many of these star performers. Why? Past fund performance is often a rotten guide to future results. Investors sometimes review past performance and then simply presume it will persist into the future. This can be a terrible mistake. The fact is that identifying funds that will perform well in the future is a lot tougher than finding funds that did well in the past.

While past performance should clearly be a major factor in picking funds, there are other factors that you should also consider:

- Can you get into and out of the fund without paying a sales commission?
- Does the fund have moderate annual expenses?
- Is there some likelihood that the fund's past performance

will persist into the future? Or was the fund's stellar track record the result of one or two exceptional years that are unlikely to be repeated?

▪ Has the fund fundamentally changed, for example because the fund manager has quit or because the fund has grown dramatically in size?

The significance of these four questions—and how you can get answers to them—is the subject of the next three chapters.

7

Loaded Questions: Why You Should Never Pay a Sales Commission

The fund industry now offers well over 3,000 mutual funds, many of them extraordinarily specialized. There are funds for Muslims, Lutherans, and those with social consciences. General Electric employees, doctors, and members of the American Association of Retired Persons all have funds that they can call their own. There are funds for people who want to invest in food and agriculture stocks, companies in the Northwest, or tax-exempt municipal bonds in North Carolina. There is even a fund that has more than a quarter of its assets in a Philippines gold- and copper-mining company.

How does an investor go about choosing from among all these funds? To some extent, you have already started to choose. You are interested in stocks, which narrows the field to some 1,400 funds. You are especially interested in funds that allow you to buy into the various investment styles described in chapters 4 and 5. That further narrows the list, to some 1,100 funds. And, of course, you want funds with good track records compared with other funds that use simi-

lar investment styles. Despite what the mutual fund market-
ers would have you believe, not all of these 1,100 funds can
legitimately claim to be top performers.

Load Versus No-Load Funds

Now is the time to do some more pruning. Mutual funds
basically fall into two categories, those that are sold through
brokers, financial planners, and insurance agents and charge
a sales commission, and those that can be bought directly
from fund groups and levy little or nothing in the way of a
sales commission. (Sales commissions are also known as
sales charges or sales loads.)

By using a broker or some other type of securities salesman, you won't necessarily end up with a better fund. In
terms of average performance, there is no difference between
the funds that charge a sales commission and those that
don't. Both sets of funds boast their fair share of star performers, as well as a good number of turkeys. A broker's advice
can be extremely helpful in sorting through these funds, and
thus for the financially naive it may be worth paying a sales
commission when buying a fund.

But if you are willing to do even a modest amount of
work—such as reading a tedious book on mutual funds—
then it is possible to make intelligent fund selections without
paying a sales commission. By doing that, you will already
have a head start on the vast majority of fund buyers. Two-
thirds of all stock and bond fund assets are in broker-sold
funds. These funds can charge up-front sales commissions
as high as 8.5%. That means that for every $1,000 invested,
only $915 goes to work for you in the fund. The rest goes to
the brokerage firm.

By avoiding these load funds and instead sticking with no-
load funds, you can ensure that when you invest $1,000, the
full $1,000 will be invested on your behalf. Over time,
avoiding sales commissions can boost your returns substan-

tially, provided you do a reasonably good job of picking funds. If you invested $1,000 in an 8.5% load fund and the fund returns 10% a year over the next decade, your money would grow to $2,373. But if instead you chose a no-load fund which also returned 10% a year, your money after 10 years would be worth almost $2,594—over $220 more than with the load fund.

The Dreaded 12b-1

Over the past decade, many funds have introduced a new annual charge known as a 12b-1 fee, which is named after a Securities and Exchange Commission rule. A 12b-1 fee is an annual charge that cuts into your return just like any of the fund's other annual expenses. Some no-load funds levy 12b-1 fees of around 0.25% of assets annually, or 25 cents for every $100 invested. In these instances, the fee is used to pay for costs like advertising and literature sent to fund shareholders. If a fund doesn't charge a sales commission and it has an annual 12b-1 fee of 0.5% or less, you should consider buying it, just as you would a pure no-load fund.

But be careful. These no-load funds shouldn't be confused with broker-sold funds that charge 12b-1 fees in conjunction with an upfront or back-end sales commission. Many broker-sold stock funds, for instance, have revamped their fee structure in recent years so that investors pay a 5.75% up-front sales commission, instead of the maximum 8.5%. But to compensate brokers for the drop in the front-end sales charge, these funds now levy an annual 0.25% 12b-1 fee, which is used to provide ongoing compensation to the broker who sold the fund.

Other broker-sold funds don't charge any upfront sales commission. Instead, they get their sales fee by charging 12b-1 fees of, say, 0.75% annually. To the novice investor, these funds can look like no-load funds. Indeed, some unscrupulous brokers have apparently pitched the funds that way. But not only do these funds levy a hefty 12b-1 fee, they also hit you hard if you bail out of the fund before the end of a specified time period, normally five or six years. Depending on how quickly you jump ship, you can get hit with a back-end sales charge of as much as 6%. To find out exactly what sales commission and annual fees a fund charges, look in the fund's prospectus. A table spelling out the various fees involved usually appears near the front of the document.

The Bottom Line: If You Use a Broker, You'll Pay

Broker-sold fund groups are constantly tinkering with their funds' commission structures. Partly that reflects an effort to make the business of selling mutual funds less like hawking cars, where the salesman gets his commission and that is the end of it, and more like a service business, where the broker gets ongoing compensation in return for making sure that his clients are satisfied and stick with their fund investments.

But the side effect is that there is often little or nothing in the way of an upfront sales commission on many broker-sold funds, so investors who want to avoid sales charges have to be especially careful. A broker who sells a fund is going to get compensated in some way or another. So if you buy a fund from a broker, you have to expect to pay some sort of fee, even if the nature of that fee isn't immediately apparent.

All insurance agents, and many financial planners, sell load funds, just as a broker would. But there is a growing group of so-called fee-only financial planners, who will recommend no-load funds in return for an hourly consultation fee or for a fee that is based on the amount of money you are investing.

I believe the vast majority of investors should be able to pick funds on their own. But if you really need professional assistance, using a fee-only financial planner is probably the best route, because these financial planners don't have the conflicts of interest that a broker has. It is in a broker's best interest, for instance, to recommend a fund that pays him or her the highest sales commission. That is not the case with a fee-only financial planner.

And Even If You Don't Use a Broker, You Might Still Pay

It is not just broker-sold funds that charge sales commissions. So too do some fund groups, such as Dreyfus Corp. and Fidelity Investments, which sell most or all of their funds directly to the public. These fund groups offer a mix of funds, some of which are no-load and some of which charge commissions of up to 3%. But rather than going to a broker, this 3% sales charge goes to the fund management company and is, in essence, another source of profit for the fund group. Because some of their funds carry small sales charges, Dreyfus and Fidelity are often known as low-load fund groups. (In addition, Fidelity and Dreyfus have other funds that were launched with the intention that they would be sold through brokers; these funds charge more than 3%.)

Is it worth paying the 3%? Many claim that it is. Their favorite argument: the case of Fidelity Magellan Fund, which charges a 3% upfront fee. Under the stewardship of the now-retired Peter Lynch, Magellan put together one of the fund industry's most astonishing long-term track records. Would it have been worth paying 3% for Magellan? Sure it would, providing you could have been assured that Lynch would do as well in the future as he had done in the past. But the stellar record is apparent only in hindsight. At any moment, even the best fund manager can lose his knack or decide to retire, and the fund's performance can go steadily downhill.

A case in point: 44 Wall Street Fund. It ranked as the fund industry's third-best-performing fund during the 1970s, with a gain of 392.1%. But in the 1980s, the fund's total return was an abysmal −73.1%, making it the poorest-performing mutual fund tracked by Lipper Analytical Services. Given the chance that a fund's performance may go off the rails, it doesn't make sense to further stack the odds against yourself by paying a 3% commission. For every top fund manager who runs a fund that carries a sales charge, there is usually somebody who is at least as good who runs a no-load mutual fund with a comparable investment strategy.

8

Counting the Pennies: Stacking the Odds in Your Favor with Low-cost Funds

If you avoid funds that charge a sales commission, the world of mutual funds suddenly narrows considerably. Lipper Analytical Services calculates that there are some 400 diversified stock funds that don't charge a sales commission of any sort. To pare this list even further, let's take a look at the other costs incurred by fund investors: turnover costs, taxes, and the fund's management fee and other annual expenses.

Among money market funds and bond funds, variations in expenses are the major factor that distinguishes the performance of one fund from another (this will be discussed in chapter 15). But with stock funds, costs—though important—are not the most crucial consideration. The reason: Stock fund returns can vary enormously, even among funds that use essentially the same investment style. If you buy a lousy stock fund, you will get lousy performance, no matter how low the expenses are. The trick with stock funds is to ensure that expenses aren't so outlandish that they over-whelm returns.

The Fund Manager's Cut

The easiest cost to consider is a fund's annual expenses, formally known as the fund's expense ratio. Expressed as a percentage, this usually ranges between 0.2% and 2%. What this percentage reflects is the past year's annual expenses as a percentage of fund assets. Thus a 1.31% expense ratio means the fund ran up annual expenses of $1.31 for every $100 it had under management. Included in expenses are things like the management fee paid to the fund's investment adviser, 12b-1 fees, and the cost of servicing shareholder accounts. Like fund sales charges, a fund's annual expense ratio is disclosed near the front of the prospectus. And like sales commissions, high annual expenses can put a signifi-cant dent in your returns.

Imagine two funds, one with a 1% expense ratio and the other with a 2% expense ratio. Both funds return 10% a year over 10 years—before expenses are deducted. Figure in expenses and the thriftier fund would turn $1,000 into $2,367 over the 10-year period, while the more costly fund would grow to just $2,159. Thus, everything else being equal, you should opt for the lower-cost fund.

Clearly, it is foolish to buy a rotten fund just because it has low expenses. But it also makes no sense to buy a good fund with high expenses. If you take the time to shop around, you will find that there are plenty of well-run funds with modest annual expenses.

On average, stock funds charge expenses of around 1.5% annually. As a rule, avoid funds that charge expenses higher than that. The two exceptions are international funds and small-company funds, which tend to have somewhat higher annual expenses. But even with these funds, you should steer clear of funds with expenses of over 2%—and if you hunt

around, you should be able to find funds with far lower
expenses than that.

Don't Just Do Something, Sit There

Turnover costs are a thornier issue. A fund's turnover
reflects the amount of buying and selling that a fund manager
does. If you dig into a fund's prospectus or a fund's annual
report, you can find the turnover figure. Sometimes turnover
can change dramatically from one year to the next, so you
might want to look at the numbers for the past three years.

A 100% turnover rate means that, over the past year, a
fund bought and sold stock equivalent to the entire size of
the fund's portfolio. A 50% turnover rate means the fund
turned over only half its portfolio during the year, implying
that it typically holds a stock for around two years. A 200%
turnover rate, meanwhile, means that over the past year the
fund has traded stocks equal to twice the size of the fund's
portfolio, which suggests that its average holding period is
around six months. On average, stock funds have annual
turnover of around 90%, implying an average holding period
of a little over a year.

Growth-stock funds typically have higher turnover than
value funds, so if you choose to ignore funds with high turnover, you may end up missing out on some of the better
growth funds. Nonetheless, be leery of funds that have turnover of more than 200% a year. Why? Because every time a
fund buys or sells a stock, it costs you money. For starters,
the fund has to pay brokerage commissions. The amount
paid in commissions is an additional cost that is not included
in the fund's annual expenses. But the sums involved are
relatively slight compared to the unseen costs of trading.
These unseen costs consist of two components.

First, there is the so-called bid-ask spread. This is a particular issue with stocks that are quoted on the Nasdaq stock
quotation system. A slew of Wall Street firms make markets

in the stocks that are quoted on the Nasdaq system. These firms stand ready to buy and sell certain stocks in which they make a market; the price at which they are willing to sell is typically somewhat higher than the price at which they are willing to buy. Thus if you simultaneously bought and sold a particular stock, you would suffer a small loss.

There is a second unseen cost of trading. If a fund is a big buyer or seller of stock, or if it trades in relatively illiquid markets where there is not a lot of trading volume, then the fund's own buying and selling can cause the price of the stock to move. This can be a particular problem for three types of funds: those that are very large, with $1 billion or more in assets; those that invest in foreign markets; and those that dabble in smaller-company stocks.

A fund, for instance, might try to buy 20,000 shares of an infrequently traded stock. But at the current market price, only 5,000 shares are being offered for sale. To attract more sellers, the market maker for the stock raises the stock's price. The fund manager, if he wants to buy more than 5,000 shares, is compelled to pay a higher price, thereby making it more expensive for the fund to accumulate the desired stock position. Similarly, if a fund tries to sell a large block of stock, this can drive down the stock's price, so that the fund manager ends up receiving a lower price than he had originally hoped for.

The Tax Man Cometh

There is a third expense that investors have to consider—taxes. Some funds generate far bigger annual distributions than others. But rather than simply avoiding these funds, you should try to avoid paying taxes—by owning these funds through a tax-deferred investment vehicle like an IRA or a 401(k) plan. You can put only $2,000 into an IRA each year, and there are similar (though higher) limits on the amounts you can put into a company-sponsored retirement plan.

Given those contribution limits, you should be picky about which sorts of funds you use for these tax-deferred investment vehicles.

Which funds should you hold in your IRA or 401(k) plan? The prime candidates are funds that buy stocks with high dividend yields, because these funds end up making big income distributions each year. In this camp, the biggest culprits are often value funds, especially those classified as equity-income funds. If you plan to buy a fund like Lindner Dividend Fund, T. Rowe Price Equity-Income Fund, or Vanguard Equity-Income Fund, consider doing it through your IRA.

What about funds that make big capital gains distributions each year? That is far trickier. If a fund buys high-dividend-yielding stocks, it is going to make big income distributions, regardless of what is going on in the market. But the size of capital gains distributions is far less predictable.

The conventional wisdom is that funds with high turnover, like aggressive growth funds, realize their gains quickly and therefore make big capital gains distributions each year. But in practice, this often isn't the case. These funds may, for instance, be attracting a lot of new money from shareholders. As a consequence, gains made earlier in the year are spread over a far larger asset base by the time it comes to make the year-end capital gains distribution.

Conversely, low-turnover funds are often pegged as tax-efficient, because they are slow to sell stocks and thus realize their gains. But unless these funds decide to hold onto their stocks forever, those gains will eventually be realized—and when they are, there will be some fat tax bills to be paid. Pity the poor shareholder who happens to buy the fund in the year when those gains are realized. He will be hit with a sizable tax bill, even though he has only just bought into the fund.

But there is one group of low-turnover funds where you can be sure you won't experience this problem—index funds. These funds simply buy and hold the securities that make up a particular market index, like the Standard & Poor's 500 stock index or the Wilshire 5000 index. By buying many or all the stocks that make up a particular market index, an index fund aims to produce gains or losses that are identical to that of the market index. The only time an index fund sells a stock is if the stock gets dropped from the index, a relatively rare occurrence. Because index funds generate only modest capital gains distributions, you may want to hold these funds in regular, taxable accounts, rather than owning them in an IRA or 401(k) plan. Instead, for your IRA or 401(k) plan, use actively managed stock funds, especially those favoring high-dividend-paying stocks.

Avoiding fund sales commissions and holding down costs like expenses, turnover, and taxes are ways of stacking the odds in your favor. But costs are just one component of a stock fund's performance. In effect, the performance of your stock fund portfolio will hinge on two key factors: how your funds perform in the future and what it costs to get that performance. Costs, while relatively easy to gauge, are not the most important consideration. Future performance is. That is where we will turn next.

9

Kicking the Tires: Making Sure a Top-Performing Fund Is Likely to Stay That Way

You have identified some top-performing funds. You have figured out which of the five investment styles is used by each fund. You have then compared each fund's record to those of other funds with a comparable investment style. You have also made sure that the funds meet the various cost criteria.

The next step: kicking the tires, trying to ensure that there is some likelihood that a fund's stellar past performance will continue into the future. Just because a fund has soared over the past decade doesn't mean it will sparkle during the next 10 years. How do you know which funds will shine and which will falter?

There are three danger signals to watch for. First, sometimes a fund has done well only because of one or two lucky calls that are unlikely to be repeated. Second, the fund may have a great record, but the fund manager responsible for the record may have retired or quit. Finally, a fund occasionally changes dramatically, either because of a rapid growth in fund assets or because of a change in investment style. All three of these potential problems can be easily checked out.

Problem Number 1: Lucky Managers

To get around the problem of lucky fund managers, look at a fund's track record on a year-by-year basis. Many funds have been launched in the last five or six years; others date back to the 1920s. If a fund's track record is long enough, try to get 10 years of data. A fund group's phone rep should be able to give you this information. The annual performance numbers may also be available in the fund's prospectus or in some of the publications mentioned in chapter 3.

Why is the year-by-year breakdown so important? Some funds have good long-term records, but only because they had one or two fabulous years, which may have come about due to luck more than skill. In looking at a fund's record on a year-by-year basis, it is helpful to know how a broad stock market average, like the Standard & Poor's 500 stock index, did in each of these years. If you go back to table 2, you can see how the S&P 500 stocks performed from 1973 to 1992. If the S&P 500 is up 32%, as it was in 1980, 1985, and 1989, then investors shouldn't be surprised if a stock fund posted a similar sort of gain in that year.

Of more concern are funds whose long-term track record is based on a couple of years when the fund's performance was way out of whack with the market averages. At the end of 1990, for instance, Mathers Fund ranked as one of the fund industry's top five-year performers, with a total return of 100.8%, making it the 47th-best performer out of 865 stock funds tracked by Lipper Analytical Services. But Mathers didn't achieve that distinction through consistently good performance year in and year out. Instead, the record was built on two well-timed moves out of stocks and into cash.

Those two switches allowed the fund to post healthy gains in 1987 and 1990, two years that were dreadful for most other stock funds.

So is it a good idea to buy the Mathers Fund? Probably not. If you ignore 1987 and 1990, the record of the Mathers Fund is mediocre. Unless the fund continues to make astute switches in and out of the stock market—an unlikely possibility—Mathers probably won't maintain its position near the top of the five-year performance charts.

Owning funds with consistent performance has another benefit. While you should avoid putting money into stocks that you will need in the near future, occasionally situations arise where you are forced to sell a part of your portfolio quickly. If you own highly volatile funds, which bounce up and down sharply with every market movement, you could end up selling fund shares at deeply depressed prices if you are compelled to bail out during a bear market. By looking at a fund's record on a year-by-year basis, you will get a sense of just how bad a fund's performance can be in any given year. In particular, it is worth looking at a fund's record in years like 1981, 1984, 1987, and 1990, when most stock funds either posted modest gains or suffered losses. Funds with good bear market performance have the added virtue of giving comfort to skittish investors who find market downturns unnerving.

Problem Number 2: Managers Who Jump Ship

After checking out the consistency of a fund's record, you next need to call the fund group involved and make sure the stock-picker responsible for the fund's record is still at the fund's helm. Most funds are run using the star system, in which a single portfolio manager is largely responsible for the fund's performance. In recent years, there has been a sharp increase in the number of fund managers who have jumped ship for one reason or another. Often top managers are lured away from big fund groups by the chance to have an ownership stake in a smaller money management firm.

In most cases, if a fund manager jumps ship, so should you. There are a lot of decent funds available, so it makes little sense to stick with a fund that has a new manager of uncertain ability. If you already own a fund, make a point of calling once a year to check that your fund's manager hasn't quit or retired. Fund groups are getting better about informing shareholders when there is a change in portfolio manager, but it pays to double-check.

Most stock funds are run by a single portfolio manager, but not all. There are other ways of managing funds that are far less dependent on any one stock-picker, and investors in these funds don't have to worry as much about personnel changes. Some funds, like the Dodge & Cox funds or the Twentieth Century funds, use a team approach. Other funds rely heavily on computerized stock selection systems. That is the case, for instance, with Vanguard Quantitative Portfolios and Vanguard Trustees' Commingled Fund–International Portfolio. Computers also play a big part in Twentieth Century's stock selection.

A few fund groups are starting to experiment with the multiple manager system. That is when a fund's assets are divided among two, three, four, or even more stock-pickers, who each run their portion of the fund as a separate portfolio. By using a group of managers, a fund can generate more consistent performance—and fund investors need worry less about manager changes. Capital Research & Management, a broker-sold fund group, has successfully used the multiple manager system for many years. More recently, Vanguard Group has started to adopt such a system for some of its funds.

Of all the different types of stock funds, index funds are least affected by manager changes. Index funds, which simply seek to replicate the performance of a particular market index, don't involve any active stock-picking, so there is no danger posed by the departure of the fund's manager.

Problem Number 3: Burgeoning Fund Assets

The tests described in the last few chapters—the cost tests, comparing the fund's record to other funds with the same investment style, looking at the fund's long-term performance and also the year-by-year breakdown, and checking that the fund's manager hasn't changed—are the most crucial. But it is probably worth making one final check. Very occasionally funds switch their investment style, either by choice or because the fund has grown so big that it is forced to change the way it operates. Vanguard Small Capitalization Stock Fund used to be an actively managed fund. It performed poorly through much of the 1980s. In 1989, the fund switched investment strategies, becoming an index fund that seeks to track the performance of the Russell 2000 index of smaller-company stocks. Because of the switch, its record before 1989 became meaningless.

For small-company stock funds, a rapid growth in fund assets can be especially problematic. Some popular funds like T. Rowe Price New Horizons Fund, the granddaddy of small-stock funds with more than $1 billion in assets, are now so big that, while the fund may perform well, it is unlikely to deliver topflight results. Why is big bad? As explained in the last chapter, the unseen costs of trading become a significant issue for a large fund. Because the fund is typically buying and selling in large quantities, its own actions can move the price of a stock, so that the fund may end up paying more to acquire stock and receiving less when it sells.

In addition, it is difficult for a large fund to get a meaningful position in the stock of a smaller company. Funds normally avoid owning more than 10% of any one company's stock. Thus, if a fund manager spots a wonderful company with a stock market value of $80 million, he would probably buy no

more than $8 million of that company's stock; in all likeli-
hood, he wouldn't go above $4 million. A $4 million position
would be significant for a fund with $100 million in assets,
but it would hardly make a dent in a fund with $1 billion in
assets. As a result, investors should probably avoid buying
small-stock funds that grow above $300 million in assets and
large-stock funds that grow above $3 billion.

If you are already invested in a fund that grows above
those levels, you should be alert to any deterioration in the
fund's performance relative to its peers. But the fact that a
fund grows fairly large shouldn't necessarily be taken as a
sell signal.

Investors should also be leery of funds that grow too
quickly, because rapid growth can disrupt the way a fund is
run. If a large-company stock fund has doubled in size over
the past 12 months, investors should think twice before investing in the fund unless the fund's assets are, say, less than
$1 billion in total. Unfortunately, you can't be quite so picky
when selecting a small-company stock fund. Any small-stock
fund with decent performance is likely to enjoy a rapid influx
of money at some point; if you can find a top-notch small-
stock fund with assets of less than $300 million, consider
buying it, even if the fund is growing rapidly in size. To check
on a fund's asset growth, or on any switch in investment
style, talk to one of the fund's phone reps.

Checking Out New Funds

With so many funds launched since the mid-1980s, investors are faced with the tricky task of trying to analyze funds
that have been introduced only recently. If a fund is brought
out by a well-regarded fund company, such as Fidelity Investments, T. Rowe Price Associates, or Twentieth Century Investors, you can have some confidence that the fund will be
reasonably well run. But even with that assurance, you still

face the prospect of buying a fund with only the very shortest of track records.

How short is too short? It is probably wise to avoid funds with track records of less than three years and to be cautious about funds that have records of less than five years. If a fund doesn't have a five-year record, the only reason to buy it is if the fund's manager has previously put together a top-notch record either by running another mutual fund or by managing money privately for wealthy clients or big institutional investors.

Unless you follow the whole money management field extremely closely, you probably won't be aware of renowned private money managers who decide to launch a mutual fund. But you may well hear about top stock-pickers who jump from one mutual fund to another, because these switches tend to generate a fair amount of publicity in the financial press.

In 1991, for instance, Dick Weiss and Carlene Murphy left Stein Roe Special Fund, where they had put together a fine long-term record, and took over the Strong Common Stock Fund. A year earlier, Stuart Roberts left Founders Funds to launch a new fund, Montgomery Small Cap Fund.

A fund manager switching funds sometimes creates an interesting opportunity for fund investors, especially if the manager ends up with a much smaller portfolio. Skilled stock-pickers running small portfolios are often able to generate spectacular short-term results, because they can be much more choosy about the stocks that they buy. Both Roberts, and Weiss and Murphy, put together fabulous results in their first year with their new smaller funds.

Putting the Rules into Practice

Picking a fund isn't simply a matter of applying a set of sacrosanct rules. Often the fund you choose will look excellent based on some criteria and not so hot based on others. For proof of that, take a look at the three small-company growth funds listed in table 3. Imagine that you were trying to pick among these funds at the start of 1993. None would be a bad choice for a portfolio. All three are no-load, boast decent track records, and still retain the stock-pickers who were responsible for the track record.

So how do you choose among them? Each fund has black marks against it. Founders Discovery Fund has high turnover, high expenses, and a short track record. Sit "New Beginning" Growth Fund looks good on expenses and turnover, but its record—while good in the 1982–87 period—hasn't been quite so impressive in recent years. Twentieth Century Ultra's record is good and its expenses are low, but by the end of 1992 the fund had clearly become pretty popular, with assets of over $5 billion. Because of that huge asset base, the fund has been compelled to invest in stocks that are relatively large, at least by the standards of most small-stock funds.

The Twentieth Century fund also shows signs of being a bear market wimp. The fund got killed in 1984 and in early 1992. But 1992's growth-stock massacre wasn't particularly kind to any of the three funds. Through the first six months of 1992, Sit "New Beginning" Growth tumbled 14.4%, Twentieth Century Ultra fell 17.2%, and Founders Discovery dropped 8.9%, according to Lipper Analytical Services. All three funds bounced back in the second half of the year.

Which should you buy? It is probably advisable to skip the Twentieth Century fund because of its size. It is just too tough to generate good returns running a big fund in the small-stock arena. The recent performance of Sit "New Beginning" Growth is troublesome. The fund's good long-term record is appealing, but investors should also give some weight to a fund's more recent performance.

The Founders fund may well be the best pick. Its small size and stellar three-year track record are pluses. Expenses

Table 3

COMPARISON SHOPPING

Below are three small-company stock funds, all of which use the growth-stock investment style.

	Founders Discovery Fund	Sit "New Beginning" Growth Fund	Twentieth Century Ultra Investors
Sales charge	none	none	none
Expense ratio	1.97%	0.83%	1.00%
Avg 3-yr turnover	190%	39%	81%
Fund assets ($mil)	$151	$325	$5,299
Fund manager's name	Michael Haines	Douglas Jones	Multiple mgrs (1981)
(year started)	(1989)	(1982)	
3-year return*	28.4%	16.6%	27.3%
5-year return*	N.A.	18.7%	26.2%
10-year return*	N.A.	17.1%	17.2%
1982	N.A.	64.2%	30.2%
1983	N.A.	26.8%	26.9%
1984	N.A.	−3.2%	−19.5%
1985	N.A.	43.7%	26.4%
1986	N.A.	10.3%	10.3%
1987	N.A.	5.5%	6.7%
1988	N.A.	9.8%	13.3%
1989	N.A.	35.2%	36.9%
1990	13.2%	−2.0%	9.4%
1991	62.5%	65.5%	86.5%
1992	15.2%	−2.1%	1.3%

*Annualized returns for periods ended December 31, 1992
N.A.: Not available; fund is too new

Source: Morningstar, Inc.

will come down as the fund grows in size. And the high
turnover? The fund is aggressive, and that high turnover is
the price you pay if you want fund manager Michael Haines
to manage your money.

If this analysis sounds straightforward and simple, it is. All
you are doing is a little comparison shopping, as you would
when choosing a microwave oven or buying a car. You don't
have to be a rocket scientist to analyze a mutual fund. A little
common sense will do just fine.

The Checklist: Finding Out Who's Naughty and Who's Nice

Before moving on to Part IV, which deals with how to put
together a stock fund portfolio, here is a quick rundown on
some of the guidelines you should use in picking stock funds:

○ Begin by drawing up a list of suspects, top-performing
funds that you have identified from sources such as adver-
tisements and fund performance surveys.
○ Sort this list into five groups based on the five investment styles: small-company growth, small-company value,
large-company growth, large-company value, and international. Start by favoring those funds with the best five-year
track records, but don't ignore newer funds.
○ Strike from your five lists any fund that charges a sales
commission.
○ Delete from the list any U.S. large-company stock fund
with annual expenses above 1.5% and any international or
small-company stock fund with an expense ratio above 2%.
○ Be leery of funds with turnover above 200%.
○ Look at a fund's record on a year-by-year basis. Ditch any
fund whose record consists of long periods of mediocre
results interspersed with brief periods of stellar performance.

○ Check to see that the stock-picker responsible for a fund's record is still at the fund's helm.
○ Avoid large-company stock funds with assets above $3 billion and small-stock funds with assets above $300 million. Also be wary of large-company stock funds that have grown 100% or more in assets over the past year.

☐PART IV☐
BUILDING A WINNING STOCK FUND PORTFOLIO

10

Recipes for Success: Four Strategies for Stock Fund Investors

Laziness is a common vice when it comes to investing. Many people end up suffering a penny-pinching retirement because they never gave serious thought to how much money they were saving or where they were saving it. College kids graduate loaded with debt because their parents never got around to putting aside money to meet ballooning college tuition costs. And even committed investors end up suffering through a lot more share-price gyrations than they really have to because they never took the time to think about the mix of investments that they own.

Partly with the lazy in mind, the four chapters that follow describe four strategies for putting together a mutual fund portfolio. As you will see, the four strategies are not mutually exclusive. You could use just strategies number 1 and 2 or you could pick elements from all four. It all depends on your disposition. If you think of investing as a necessary evil to which you wish to devote only the briefest amount of time, then the first two strategies will probably suffice. But if you consider investing to be a hobby, then you may want to draw on all four strategies.

The four strategies address only the stock fund portion of your portfolio; the role of bond and money market funds will be discussed in Part V.

What are the four strategies? Here is a quick preview.

Strategy number 1 involves putting together a portfolio of stock index funds. Index funds don't make any effort to distinguish between the merits of individual stocks. Instead, they buy only the stocks that make up a particular market index and thereby aim to mimic the index's performance. If you put together a portfolio of index funds, you can guarantee that you will do about as well as the market averages.

With strategy number 2, you get to choose among the star stock-pickers of the mutual fund industry. The idea is to build a well-diversified portfolio comprised of the best actively managed funds you can find. By picking top-notch funds, your aim is to do better than the market averages.

Strategy number 3 involves customizing your portfolio to reflect your age. If you are young, you have a long time to invest and thus can be more sanguine about day-to-day market swings. Your aim: the highest returns you can get. If you are older, you may find market volatility more unnerving because you need to live off the earnings of your portfolio. As a result, you might want to put together a more staid portfolio, where you sacrifice the chance for explosive gains because you want to avoid the risk of dramatic short-term losses.

Strategy number 4 is for mutual fund aficionados who don't mind spending extra time in an effort to get superior returns. The fourth strategy involves closed-end funds, one of the least publicized areas of the mutual fund world. Closed-end funds offer the chance to buy into the stock market at bargain prices. By astutely buying and selling these funds, you can add substantially to your returns.

You should consider using strategy number 1—the index

fund strategy—for 30% to 50% of your stock fund portfolio. The other 50% to 70% should be invested in a mix of actively managed funds, which you will choose by drawing on the other three strategies.

As you will quickly discover, combining these various strategies can involve investing in a host of funds. To put together a portfolio of index funds, you need to buy three or four funds. Building a diversified portfolio of actively managed stock funds involves investing in another five or six funds. Put it all together and you could own as many as 10 funds. This may seem excessive. After all, mutual funds are meant to make investing easier and here comes a knuckle-lehead author suggesting you buy a slew of different funds.

You could cut down the number of funds in your portfolio, either by dropping the stock index funds or by eliminating the actively managed stock funds. But either way you would lose a key component of your portfolio. The stock index funds are an anchor, guaranteeing that you will get whatever the market delivers. The actively managed stock funds are there both to help boost returns and to let you customize your portfolio to more closely suit your needs. Keeping tabs on eight or ten funds seems a small price to pay to get those benefits.

Those who feel queasy about owning so many funds may want to use the Mutual Fund Marketplace operated by Charles Schwab & Co., the San Francisco discount brokerage firm. A discount brokerage firm is a different beast from a full-service brokerage firm such as Merrill Lynch & Co. or Prudential Securities, Inc., which are in the business of selling load funds. Commissions are much lower at a discount brokerage firm, and there are no brokers to either offer advice or to pressure you into trading securities.

Investors who use Schwab's Marketplace can buy funds from roughly 100 no-load and low-load fund families. When you buy most funds through Schwab, you have to pay a small transaction fee plus the fund's load, if any. But with some of the funds offered through Schwab, such as those managed by Janus Group of Mutual Funds, Founders Funds, and Neuberger & Berman Management, there is no transaction fee.

What are the advantages of using Schwab? First, the firm provides you with consolidated account statements, relieving you of some of the paperwork involved in owning several mutual funds. Second, you can often get into funds for less than their regular investment minimum if you go through Schwab. Third, using Schwab's Marketplace can save you valuable time when making switches between funds in different fund families. Switching between funds in the Schwab Marketplace takes only a phone call. If you don't use Schwab, it can take as long as three weeks to switch between fund groups, because you first have to redeem your shares, then wait for the check to arrive, and finally send off a new check to the new mutual fund.

Other discount brokerage firms, such as Boston's Fidelity Discount Brokerage and San Diego's Jack White & Co., offer a similar service to Schwab's, but Schwab currently ranks as the leading firm in the field. Because of the transaction fees involved, you may prefer to skip the Schwab Marketplace. But for those who would otherwise resist owning multiple mutual funds because they loathe the paperwork involved, the Schwab Marketplace makes a lot of sense.

11

Strategy Number 1: The Case for Index Funds

When it comes to investing, it helps to have a little humility. Stock market investing may be one of the most lucrative games in town, but it is also one of the toughest. After all, not everybody can beat the market. As a group, stock market investors will earn returns equal to those of the stock market averages. That is an irrefutable fact. But figure in such expenses as trading costs and fees paid to professional money managers and the average investor is actually destined to lag the market.

Do you really believe you can beat the market by buying individual stocks or individual stock mutual funds? Think about that for a little while and you will realize that you are being pretty arrogant. There are thousands of professional investors, all with MBAs, fancy computers, and access to the best stock market research. These stock jockeys pore over the market each day, trying to find undervalued stocks.

When you buy a stock, you may well be buying from one

of these folks. In making that buy decision, you are making the presumption that you know more about the prospects for the company involved than the person who is selling the stock to you. And every time you sell a stock, because you think the stock is going to go down, you are making the presumption that you know better than the person who is taking the stock off your hands. It is no different with stock mutual funds. Every time you sell a fund, you are effectively selling a group of stocks. Every time you buy a fund, you are buying a group of stocks. Do you really know more than all those other bright folks in the market?

Buying the Market

But there is one surefire, slam-dunk, bullet-proof way of beating the average investor. You buy an index fund. Index funds don't employ active stock-pickers. They simply buy the stocks that make up a particular stock market index and thus seek to mimic the index's performance. The most popular index funds track the Standard & Poor's 500 stock index, an index of 500 larger-company stocks that represent around 70% of U.S. stock market value. More recently, newer index funds have been introduced that track indices like the Russell 2000 index of smaller stocks, the Standard & Poor's MidCap Index of mid-sized stocks, and the Morgan Stanley Capital International Index for Europe, Australia, and the Far East. (A list of some of the more popular index funds appears in the appendix.)

How do index funds get their edge? Index funds remain fully invested in the stock market at all times, so there is no danger that they will be left behind during a rising stock market. That's not the case with actively managed funds, which typically keep 10% of assets in money market instruments. Funds hold this cash partly to meet redemptions by departing shareholders. In addition, some fund managers sell stocks and raise cash if they believe that stock prices are likely to drop. But if stock prices rise—as they do in most years—these cash holdings act as a drag on performance.

There is a second, more important reason why index funds do better: They charge lower expenses than regular stock funds managed by professional stock-pickers. Most stock index funds charge less than 0.5% a year, compared with the 1.5% annual expenses run up by the average stock mutual fund. And because an index fund rarely sells a stock, trading costs tend to be minute. Thus if the average investor is destined to underperform the market by an amount equal to expenses, then he or she is bound to get better results with an indexing strategy, which aims to match the performance of the market averages but involves far lower expenses than those incurred by the average investor. The higher expenses of actively managed funds have a direct impact on their published performance results: Mutual fund results are calculated after deducting costs like turnover and fund management fees.

Of course, the average stock mutual fund manager may actually be smarter than the average investor, so that fund managers as a group could outperform an indexing strategy. Certain mutual fund analysts have tried to make this argument, but not convincingly so. This doesn't mean that I think efforts to beat the market are futile. A carefully selected portfolio of mutual funds should be able to do that, even if the average stock mutual fund cannot.

But that also doesn't mean that I reject the notion of indexing. Here's why. You may indeed be able to beat an indexing strategy with a well-chosen portfolio of mutual funds. But indexing still offers a major advantage—certainty. With indexing, you are certain to outperform the average investor. And because your performance will be tied to the market indices, you can be absolutely sure that one problem won't afflict your portfolio: You won't massively underperform the market averages. Indexing is, in a sense, the ultimately rational investment strategy.

You should consider using stock index funds in combination with actively managed stock funds. Because of their predictable performance relative to the market averages, index funds can provide an anchor for your portfolio, ensuring that at least a part of your portfolio is earning the returns that the market is delivering. Index funds are a portion of your portfolio you never need worry about. Whatever the market delivers—good, bad, indifferent—that is what you will receive.

As a result, the most timid investor should consider indexing up to half of his stock fund portfolio, with the other half given over to actively managed funds. Even the most adventurous should probably keep 30% of his portfolio in index funds, with the other 70% invested in actively managed funds.

Indexing is not a popular strategy in certain circles. The stock-pickers who manage mutual funds don't like it. After all, indexing is based on the notion that simply mimicking an index will do better than their intensely researched stock picks. Indexing also isn't popular with the businesspeople who run mutual fund companies. An index fund isn't nearly as profitable for them as an actively managed mutual fund, for which they can charge a fat management fee. Despite these objections, index funds have ballooned in popularity in the early 1990s.

A Game Plan for Index Fund Investors

How should you go about indexing? Among fund investors, the favorite index funds are those that track the performance of the Standard & Poor's 500 stock index. During the 1980s, the oldest and largest of the index mutual funds, Vanguard Index Trust-500 Portfolio, beat three-quarters of all stock mutual funds simply by buying and holding the stocks in the S&P 500. Numerous other S&P 500 funds have now been launched, and the funds have become hugely popular.

But be warned: If you buy an S&P 500 fund, you are not indexing the market. The S&P 500 represents about 70% of U.S. stock market value. Most of the companies in the S&P 500 are large companies, which were just the sort of stocks that did well in the 1980s. If we have a prolonged period when small stocks outperform large stocks, then S&P 500 index funds could perform relatively poorly.

That is why buying an S&P 500 fund isn't enough. You also need to have some exposure to small and medium-sized stocks. And if you want to do that, there is really only one place to go: Vanguard Group, the Valley Forge, Pennsylvania, fund group that now ranks as the country's third-largest mutual fund group. Vanguard offers a full panoply of index funds—large-stock funds, small-stock funds, international funds.

Vanguard has another major advantage. Its index funds have the lowest expenses of any index funds available to small investors. Why are Vanguard's expenses so low? The company has an ownership structure that is unique in the mutual fund industry. Vanguard is effectively owned by the shareholders of its various mutual funds. To benefit its "owners," Vanguard doesn't make a profit each year. Instead, it keeps the expense ratios on its funds to a bare minimum and thereby rewards its shareholders.

Because of this unique ownership structure, Vanguard's funds invariably have lower expenses than comparable funds offered by other fund groups. Why? These other fund groups have to make a profit each year to benefit their corporate shareholders—and these shareholders are an entirely different group from the investors in each of their funds. Most mutual fund companies are either subsidiaries of insurance companies or brokerage firms, or they are independent companies that are privately owned or publicly traded on a stock exchange.

Vanguard's low expenses haven't ensured top-notch performance for the fund group's actively managed stock funds.

But when it comes to index funds, which are simply buying and holding a fixed group of stocks, Vanguard's low expenses give its index funds an insurmountable advantage. After all, expenses are the only thing that distinguishes one index fund's performance from another.

Using Vanguard funds, there are two ways to index the market. First, you can buy the Vanguard Index Trust-Total Stock Market Portfolio, which seeks to index the Wilshire 5000. The Wilshire 5000 includes all U.S. exchange–traded stocks. Despite its name, the index is composed of far more than 5,000 stocks.

Alternatively, you can replicate the Wilshire 5000 by combining two other Vanguard funds, the 500 Portfolio and the Extended Market Portfolio. The 500 Portfolio indexes the S&P 500 and the Extended Market Portfolio indexes the Wilshire 4500, which includes all U.S. stocks outside of the S&P 500.

It makes a lot more sense to simply buy the Vanguard Total Stock Market Portfolio. But Vanguard's Extended Market Portfolio can be useful for those who are offered an S&P 500 fund as part of their company's 401(k) or profit-sharing plan, an option that many companies make available to their employees. If that is the case, you could buy your company's S&P 500 fund with your 401(k) or profit-sharing money and then invest additional money in Vanguard's Extended Market Portfolio, so that you end up indexing the whole market.

(As noted earlier, index funds are not necessarily the best funds to hold in a tax-deferred account, because they are relatively tax-efficient. But you may want to invest part of your company retirement plan money in an S&P 500 fund, either because the other investment options in the plan are unattractive or because you don't have the spare cash to invest in index funds outside of your company plan and IRA.)

In rough terms, you would need to put $3 into the Extended Market Portfolio for every $7 you have in your company's S&P 500 fund. One of Vanguard's telephone service representatives can tell you what the exact figures are. The figures depend on the relative stock market values of the S&P 500 and the Wilshire 4500, so they will change with market movements. But once you have bought the two funds in the right proportions, you won't have to make further adjustments, because their relative sizes will change along with stock market movements.

You will, however, have to be careful to maintain the correct proportions when investing additional money in your S&P 500 fund and Vanguard Extended Market fund. Call Vanguard once a year to find out what the proportions should be and then make additional investments over the next year to bring the percentages back into line.

Taking in the World

In earlier chapters, we talked about diversifying a portfolio in three ways, by buying growth and value stocks, by investing in small and large companies, and by buying U.S. and foreign stocks. If you buy an index fund, you will pick up both growth and value stocks, and if you index the entire U.S. market, you will also end up with large and small companies.

But you also want a foreign stock component. The way to get that is to invest in Vanguard International Equity Index Fund, which comes in two parts, the European Portfolio and the Pacific Portfolio. Put together in the right proportions, these two funds will replicate the Morgan Stanley Capital International Index for Europe, Australia, and the Far East. In general, you want to invest roughly equal amounts in the two funds, but the percentages will change with market movements. Again, a Vanguard phone rep can give you the correct proportions for the two funds.

As a starting point, consider putting 30% of your index fund portfolio into foreign stock funds (the reasoning behind that figure will be discussed in the next chapter). With a 30%

foreign component, the index portion of your stock portfolio might look something like this:

Vanguard Index Trust-Total Stock Market Portfolio	70%
Vanguard International Equity Index Fund-European Portfolio	15%
Vanguard International Equity Index Fund-Pacific Portfolio	15%

Alternatively, if your company offers an S&P 500 fund and you decide to use it, your portfolio might look like this:

Your company's S&P 500 fund	50%
Vanguard Index Trust-Extended Market Portfolio	20%
Vanguard International Equity Index Fund-European Portfolio	15%
Vanguard International Equity Index Fund-Pacific Portfolio	15%

Index funds may seem boring. There is something un-American about settling for average results. You won't get to boast at cocktail parties about the hot fund you own. But remember, the biggest determinant of your portfolio's success is not which stock funds you buy, but how much of your portfolio is allocated to stocks. It is the stock market itself that is the great wealth creator. With index funds, you will be guaranteed the results of this wealth-creation machine.

12

Strategy Number 2: Putting Together a Portfolio of Winners

If you put together a portfolio of index funds, you should do better than the average stock fund investor. But you will never beat the market. And that, after all, is one of the most compelling goals of the investment game.

Beating the market is the goal of strategy number 2. Like the first strategy, the second is extremely simple. The idea is to put together a portfolio of mutual funds that is well-diversified and includes the best-managed funds you can find.

We discussed how to select top-performing stock funds in chapters 6 through 9, so that part of the strategy is already known to you. In chapters 4 and 5, we talked about the different types of funds that you should own: a small-company growth fund, a small-company value fund, a large-company growth fund, a large-company value fund, and an international fund.

How should you divide your money among these funds? As a rough guide, consider having 70% of your stock portfolio in U.S. stocks and 30% in foreign stocks. The 70% U.S. portion should be divided so that 50% of your total stock fund portfolio ends up in large-company stocks and 20% in small-company stocks. These two amounts would then be equally split between growth and value managers. Thus your stock portfolio might look something like this: 25% large-company growth, 25% large-company value, 10% small-company growth, 10% small-company value, and 30% international.

The amounts allocated to the various U.S. stock funds are meant to reflect their relative importance, based on the proportion of U.S. stock market value for which they account. As such, these are intended to be neutral weightings, with no bias shown to particular investment styles.

The percentage put in international stocks is somewhat arbitrary. Studies have been conducted to determine the best mix of foreign and U.S. stocks, based both on past performance of these two groups of stocks and on their price volatility. Suggested foreign stock allocations range as high as 40% of a stock portfolio and as low as 15% or 20%. The 30% figure is, in part, merely a compromise.

But there is another reason for picking 30%. As an investor, you should be anxious not to have too much of your fortunes tied to any particular area of the stock market. For the average U.S. investor, the biggest influence on his or her portfolio's performance is almost inevitably going to be the large American companies that dominate the U.S. stock market. Indeed, when people talk about the U.S. stock market, they tend to think about the performance of one of the large-company stock indices, like the Standard & Poor's 500 stock index or the Dow Jones Industrial Average.

The 30% foreign-stock exposure, combined with the 20% small-stock component, leaves you with just half of your portfolio in the large S&P 500-type stocks. By keeping the other half of your portfolio outside of the S&P 500, you will have a cushion should these large-company stocks do poorly. In addition, by venturing into smaller stocks and foreign stocks—both of which have the potential for rapid earnings growth—you should pick up better returns than you would have enjoyed if you had stuck only with the S&P 500.

Keeping Your Balance

Once you have set up your five-fund portfolio, each year you will have to rebalance the portfolio to maintain the target percentages. For instance, there might be a particularly good year for international funds and an especially bad year for small-company funds, so that your international fund balloons to 34% of your portfolio while your two small-company funds shrivel to 8% apiece.

To get the portfolio back into balance, so that you once again have 30% in international and 10% in each of the two small-company funds, you could sell some of your international fund shares and shift the money into the small-company funds. But unless you own the funds in an IRA or a similar tax-deferred account, this can be extremely messy from a tax standpoint. To get the percentages back into line, it is much easier to simply direct additional investments to the small-company funds.

You should make a point of calculating how much your fund investments are worth as of December 31 each year. Based on that calculation, figure out what proportion of the overall portfolio is accounted for by each fund and then make additional investments over the next 12 months so that you get the proportions back into line.

Rebalancing your portfolio doesn't just keep your portfolio in the right proportions. It can also enhance returns. In order to maintain the target percentages within your portfolio, you are forced to avoid funds that have had a good run and whose area of the market may be getting overheated. At the same time, you are compelled to put money into funds that have become depressed and may be due for a rebound.

Doubling Up

When building your portfolio, resist the temptation to buy every exciting new fund you hear about. Most investors would do well to stick with just five stock funds for the non-index portion of their stock portfolio. After all, you bought three or four index funds based on chapter 11's advice and now you are considering buying five actively managed stock funds. Add a fund for your emergency money and maybe one, two, or even three bond funds, and soon you have a dozen funds to keep tabs on. For most folks, that is plenty.

But if your entire mutual fund portfolio is larger than $200,000, you may want to consider using more than five funds for the non-index portion of your stock fund portfolio. There is no necessity to do this and those who find investing a chore probably shouldn't do it. But for the committed investor, there may be a chance to improve your returns by purchasing additional funds. The idea is to keep the same percentage of your portfolio in each of the five investment styles. But in cases where it makes sense, you should split the percentage among more than one fund.

If you want to double up on your funds in any one of the five categories, look first at the international fund area. In addition to owning an international stock fund like Harbor International Fund or T. Rowe Price International Stock Fund, which invest mostly in large-company stocks, you may also want to buy a fund that invests in smaller stocks or less-developed markets. That is the specialty of funds like T. Rowe Price International Discovery Fund and Montgomery Emerging Markets Fund. If you split the 30% international portion between two funds, you probably want to keep 25%

in a large-company fund and 5% in a small-company or emerging-markets fund.

Emerging stock markets like Indonesia, Jordan, and Thailand offer the potential for huge gains. In many cases, the underlying economy is growing two or three times faster than that of the United States, thus raising the prospect of rapid earnings growth among local companies. Emerging markets are prone to wild share-price swings, but a fund like Montgomery Emerging Markets Fund partially overcomes that problem by owning stocks from a host of different countries. Because emerging markets don't move up and down in tandem, a fund that invests in a variety of markets is far less volatile than one that sticks only with one nation's stocks.

Outside of the international stock fund arena, it can also pay to double up on your funds within the other investment styles. By doubling up, you mute the effect of any one fund manager doing especially badly, though you also of course dilute the performance of a fund that does especially well. Thus, for any of the categories, there is no point in doubling up if you reckon you already own a top-notch fund. Instead, doubling up makes sense when you are having difficulty choosing a fund for one of the categories, either because you have two funds that seem equally good or because you are faced with a group of funds that all have black marks against them and you want to hedge your bets by owning a couple of them.

Keeping It in the Family

While some investors are sufficiently devoted that they don't mind dealing with a fistful of different fund groups, less energetic investors may prefer to restrict themselves to one or two fund companies. Sticking with a couple of fund groups does make it a little easier if you have a change of address or you want to switch funds. If you are moving money between two funds in the same fund group, all that is usually needed is a single phone call.

With the less energetic in mind, five portfolios are shown in table 4. Each portfolio was put together using the funds of a single fund group. The five groups used are the five largest no-load and low-load fund groups. In certain instances, a fund group doesn't have a fund that fits one of the five investment styles. In these cases, a fund from another fund group was substituted; or, if the fund group had a fund that managed to straddle more than one investment style, the allocations were adjusted. As the portfolios were put together, a preference was shown for no-load funds.

Sticking with any of the five major no-load and low-load fund groups would not be a bad choice. All offer good service, efficient record keeping, and reasonably low costs. And each of these fund companies offers at least one or two funds with excellent reputations. But many investors will find that sticking with just one fund group can be too restrictive. There is no fund company that offers top-performing funds for all five of the fund investment styles. To find top performers in all five areas, you really have to use a variety of fund groups.

If you keep all your money with one fund group, somebody may tell you that you are taking an unnecessary risk and that there is a danger that your fund could be damaged by other, unrelated events at the fund group. I got a letter in 1990 from a doctor in Santa Ana, California. He wrote: "My question is, if some or all of [the other] mutual funds [at the fund company I use] go to 'par' and be without value, could they in some way reflect on or effect the value of my government money market fund?"

There may be many things to worry about when it comes to mutual fund investing, but this sure isn't one of them. Every mutual fund is a separate company with its own board of directors. Unless your fund manager is a crook, there is no way that your fund can be affected by poor performance at

Table 4

FAMILY AFFAIRS

Dreyfus Corporation (Uniondale, NY)
25% Dreyfus Appreciation Fund (large-company growth) 25% Dreyfus Growth and Income Fund (large-company value) 20% Dreyfus New Leaders Fund (small-company) 30% Dreyfus Strategic World Investing (international)
Fidelity Investments (Boston, MA)
25% Fidelity Growth Company Fund (large-company growth) 25% Fidelity Equity-Income Fund (large-company value) 10% Fidelity Emerging Growth Fund (small-company growth) 10% Pennsylvania Mutual Fund (small-company value) 25% Fidelity Overseas Fund (international) 5% Fidelity Emerging Markets Fund (international)
T. Rowe Price Associates (Baltimore, MD)
25% T. Rowe Price Growth Stock Fund (large-company growth) 25% T. Rowe Price Equity-Income Fund (large-company value) 10% T. Rowe Price New Horizons Fund (small-company growth) 10% Neuberger and Berman Generis Fund (small-company value) 25% T. Rowe Price International Stock Fund (international) 5% T. Rowe Price International Discovery Fund (international)
Scudder Funds (Boston, MA)
25% Scudder Capital Growth Fund (large-company growth) 25% Scudder Value Fund (large-company value) 10% Scudder Development Fund (small-company growth) 10% Nicholas II (small-company value) 30% Scudder International Fund (international)
Vanguard Group (Valley Forge, PA)
25% Vanguard World Fund-U.S. Growth Portfolio (large-company growth) 25% Vanguard Windsor II (large-company value) 10% Vanguard Explorer Fund (small-company growth) 10% Nicholas II (small-company value) 30% Vanguard World Fund-International Growth Portfolio (international)

another fund or by financial trouble at the fund's investment adviser.

Looking After the Kids

Just as you should put together a portfolio to fund your own retirement, so you may want to buy stock funds to finance your children's college education.

If you are looking to stash away money for college, consider setting up mutual fund accounts under your state's Uniform Gifts to Minors Act (UGMA) or Uniform Transfers to Minors Act (UTMA). By doing so, you will get both a tax savings and a low-cost way of getting into mutual funds.

For UGMA or UTMA accounts held by children under age 14, the first $600 of gains is currently tax-free and the next $600 is taxed at the child's tax rate. Above $1,200, investment earnings are taxed at the parents' tax rate. These break points are indexed to inflation and thus should rise over time. Children who are 14 and older are taxed at their own tax rate, usually 15%.

Some fund groups will give you a break on their investment minimum if you set up UGMA or UTMA accounts. Founders Funds and Vanguard Group, for instance, will let you establish a child's account with just $500, T. Rowe Price Associates will let you in for $1,000, and Babson Fund Group, Janus Group, Neuberger & Berman, Strong Funds, and Twentieth Century Investors will lower their minimums to $250. Some of these fund groups will also waive their minimums entirely, as long as you agree to automatically invest $25, $50, or $100 a month.

Fidelity Investments, which regularly has a $2,500 minimum on its funds, will let UGMA and UTMA accounts be opened for $1,000. The program is restricted to four funds— Fidelity Cash Reserves, Fidelity Blue Chip Growth Fund, Fidelity Asset Manager, and Fidelity Growth & Income Portfolio. Under the program, all four funds can be bought without paying a sales commission. For UGMA and UTMA accounts, Scudder Funds will lower its investment minimum from $1,000 to $500, providing you agree to invest at least $50 every month.

Money placed in UGMA or UTMA accounts becomes the property of the child. Once the kid reaches the age of majority, which in most states is 18 or 21, he or she can do whatever they want with the money; that may mean buying a new car instead of a college education. Given that possibility, should you use UGMA and UTMA accounts? It's a tricky issue. Here is one strategy you might want to consider:

If your youngster is under age 14, start by investing regularly in mutual funds held in UGMA or UTMA accounts. Build up these accounts until they are worth around $12,000. Once you hit $12,000, the funds should be kicking off close to $1,200 a year in income and capital gains distributions, which is the total amount that currently receives preferential tax treatment if your child is under age 14. As a result, if your child is still under age 14, there is not much point in putting more money into the child's mutual funds, because you won't get any additional tax savings. If you want to save further money for your child, put it into an account registered in your own name. That way you can keep control over the money, which may turn out to be wise if your kid turns out to be a monster.

Once your child turns 14, all money held by the child gets taxed at the child's tax rate, which will usually be lower than the parents' tax rate. At that point, you may want to make further contributions to your child's mutual fund accounts, including giving a gift of any money you have been saving in your own name. But if you do that, you have to be pretty confident that your delightful teenager isn't going to blow the money on a new Porsche as soon as he or she turns 18.

Funds for Their Future

If you don't have a lot of money and you want to start saving for your child's education, one strategy is to combine the Babson funds with the Twentieth Century funds. Twentieth Century's stock funds use an aggressive growth-stock style, while the Babson funds are more value-oriented. By investing $2,500 in UGMA or UTMA accounts at both fund groups, you could put together a diversified fund portfolio. Here's how:

25% ($625) Twentieth Century Growth Investors (large-company growth)
25% ($625) Babson Value Fund (large-company value)
10% ($250) Twentieth Century Vista Investors (small-company growth)
10% ($250) Babson Enterprise Fund II (small-company value)
30% ($750) Babson-Stewart Ivory International Fund (international)

If buying all those funds seems like a lot of work for a small portfolio, consider indexing instead. For just $500, you can index the entire U.S. market by buying the Vanguard Total Stock Market Portfolio in an UGMA or UTMA account. But the Vanguard fund charges a $10 annual service fee, equal to 2% on a $500 investment. Throw in the fund's 0.21% expense ratio and you end up spending 2.21% a year to index, which is a steep price to pay. Thus you probably shouldn't go the indexing route unless you plan to build up the size of your child's account fairly quickly.

If you would prefer to try something more adventurous than indexing, consider three other one-fund solutions: Fidelity Asset Manager Growth, T. Rowe Price Spectrum Growth Fund, and Vanguard STAR Fund. All three funds provide an easy way to acquire a well-diversified portfolio of securities.

T. Rowe Price Spectrum Growth Fund may be the best choice among the three funds, because it keeps a high percentage of its portfolio invested in the stock market. The T. Rowe Price fund keeps the bulk of its assets in a mixture of U.S. large-company stocks, U.S. small-company stocks, and foreign stocks. The fund achieves that mix by buying seven other T. Rowe Price funds. While not all seven funds can legitimately claim to be top performers, the fund should still appeal to those looking for a low-cost way of buying a diversified portfolio.

Just as T. Rowe Price Spectrum Growth Fund owns other T. Rowe Price funds, so Vanguard STAR Fund buys other Vanguard funds. More than 60% of the Vanguard fund's assets are given over to a mix of large- and small-company stock funds, with bond and money funds accounting for the rest of the fund's assets. Neither Vanguard STAR nor T. Rowe Price Spectrum Growth charge any annual expenses. But investors still end up paying annual fees, because they incur the expenses of the funds bought by T. Rowe Price Spectrum Growth and Vanguard STAR.

Fidelity Asset Manager Growth will generally have around 65% of its assets in stocks, though the percentage can vary depending on whether the fund's manager thinks stocks are attractively priced. There is a more subdued version of Fidelity Asset Manager Growth known as Fidelity Asset Manager, for which the minimum is $1,000 if you open a child's account. But with Fidelity Asset Manager Growth, Fidelity's regular $2,500 minimum applies.

13

Strategy Number 3: Customizing a Portfolio to Suit Your Age

Every investor is different. Some are risk-adverse, meaning that their biggest fear is losing their shirt. Others are more aggressive, meaning that their fondest hope is to make big bucks. Your own attitude toward making and losing money will depend partly on individual temperament. But age is probably an even more important factor.

If your portfolio loses 30% of its value, that isn't a big deal if you are 40 years old, are gainfully employed, and don't plan to retire for another 20 or 25 years. After all, you are not depending on your portfolio to pay day-to-day living expenses. If the market collapses, there is plenty of time for your portfolio's value to recover and go higher.

That just isn't the case if you are 70 years old and trying to live off your savings. While you probably don't expect to cash in your entire portfolio over the next year, you may be looking to consume, say, 5% of your savings during the course of the next 12 months. It is both emotionally and financially painful to sell when prices are down 30%.

The fact is that the relative importance of risk and reward change as you approach retirement and later quit the work-force. For a younger investor, reward is everything. But for a retiree, risk—meaning market-price gyrations—is much more important. That is why, as you grow older, you may want gradually to boost your bond fund holdings (the subject of chapter 17).

But there is another way for older investors to make their portfolio more tranquil: Buy a less explosive mix of stock funds. This is the essence of the third of our four portfolio-building strategies.

Strategy number 3 should be used in conjunction with the strategy described in the last chapter. As with the second strategy, you still want to put together a diversified portfolio that includes the best stock funds you can buy. But with the third strategy, you also change your stock fund mix as you grow older.

There are three ways to do that. First, you could try to buy more tranquil funds within each of the five fund categories. Second, you can cut back your investment in volatile funds like small-stock funds and foreign-stock funds and boost your position in large-company stock funds. Finally, you could downplay growth-stock funds and invest more money in sedate value funds. The first two strategies make a lot of sense. For reasons given below, I wouldn't use the last of these three strategies.

Fast Funds, Slow Funds

As a first step in customizing your portfolio to reflect your age, you might want to pick individual funds that are more or less aggressive. An older investor would want to look for funds that emphasize a company's dividend payout when picking stocks, because these funds don't tend to bounce around in price quite so violently. Younger investors, on the other hand, don't need dividend income and should instead look for funds that stress capital growth as their main objective.

A fund company's marketing literature will often make it clear just how aggressive each fund is. Twentieth Century Investors, for instance, offers six U.S. growth-stock funds. Twentieth Century's Select and Heritage funds focus on dividend-paying stocks, while Twentieth Century Giftrust, Growth, Ultra, and Vista don't worry about dividends when picking stocks. Aggressive investors should consider one of the latter four funds, while conservative investors may want to stick with Select or Heritage.

Alternatively, you might want to see how a fund did in years like 1981, 1984, 1987, and 1990, which were rough years for the market. In those years, funds typically posted only modest gains or even lost money. If a fund consistently loses money in turbulent years for the market, conservative investors may want to avoid the fund, even if it has a good long-term record.

Reshuffle Your Stock Fund Holdings

A second strategy is to change your allocations to various types of funds. A 30- or 40-year-old investor, because of his relative youth and thus long time horizon, might want to overweight small-company stocks and international stocks in the hope of earning greater returns. Older investors, by contrast, might want to put more emphasis on large-company growth and value funds. These more conservative funds have historically posted lower returns, but they also don't jump around so much in price.

If you plan to change your stock fund mix as you grow older, take as a starting point the percentages outlined in chapter 12. How far should you stray from these initial percentages? As a rule, don't allow the combined worth of your large-company growth fund and your large-company value fund to get above 60% of your total stock fund portfolio. You also shouldn't allow the value of these two large-stock funds to fall below 40%. With the two small-company funds, don't let these funds grow above 30% nor let them fall below 10%. And you should probably keep your international fund holdings at between 20% and 40% of your stock portfolio. Thus your stock fund portfolio would be constrained by the following limits:

	Maximum Holding	Neutral Holding	Minimum Holding
Large-company stock funds	60%	50%	40%
Small-company stock funds	30%	20%	10%
International stock funds	40%	30%	20%

Within these constraints, you can build a portfolio that will more closely fit your needs for higher long-term returns or greater price stability. Some "age-adjusted" stock fund portfolios are shown in table 5 on page 112. (In chapter 17, we'll look at what a mix of stock and bond funds would look like.) You shouldn't simply replicate these portfolios. Rather, use them as a starting point for putting together your own portfolio based on factors like your age, the amount you have to save, the investment options available through your company's retirement plan, and your tolerance for stock market price swings.

If you are investing money for a child's college education, your kid's portfolio should probably resemble that shown for the 50-year-old. That may not seem to make sense, given the young age of your child. But in all likelihood you will only have 18 years to save for a kid's college education, and in the final five years before college, you will be moving money into bonds. As a result, you shouldn't be too aggressive in your stock fund selection.

For the three portfolios in table 5, it is not just the

weightings for each style that have been varied. In some cases, the funds have also been varied with an eye to including more aggressive funds in the 35-year-old's portfolio and more conservative funds in the 65-year-old's portfolio. For instance, the 35-year-old's portfolio includes Twentieth Century Vista Investors, which is far more aggressive than Strong Opportunity Fund, which is in the 65-year-old's portfolio. Other funds are harder to distinguish. For example, Scudder International Fund, which is included in the 65-year-old's portfolio, is about as volatile as T. Rowe Price International

Table 5

CHANGING WITH THE TIMES

35-year-old
20% IAI Stock Fund (large-company growth) 20% Yacktman Fund (large-company value) 13% Twentieth Century Vista Investors (small-company growth) 13% Neuberger & Berman Genesis Fund (small-company value) 29% Harbor International Fund (international) 5% Montgomery Emerging Markets Fund (international)
50-year-old
25% Gabelli Growth Fund (large-company growth) 25% Neuberger & Berman Guardian Fund (large-company value) 10% Columbia Special Fund (small-company growth) 10% Babson Enterprise Fund II (small-company value) 30% T. Rowe Price International Stock Fund (international)
65-year-old
30% Financial Industrial Income Fund (large-company growth) 30% Lindner Fund (large-company value) 8% Strong Opportunity Fund (small-company growth) 8% Pennsylvania Mutual Fund (small-company value) 24% Scudder International Fund (international)

Stock Fund, which was slotted into the 50-year-old's portfolio.

Indexing a portion of your portfolio will mute the impact of the actively managed funds. As a result, you may want to make somewhat bigger bets with your actively managed funds.

Suppose, for instance, that you have a $100,000 portfolio. Half the portfolio is in Vanguard index funds and the other half is in actively managed funds. Now imagine that, because you are only in your 20s and 30s, you want to make a 30% (or $30,000) bet on small-company stock funds.

The index portion of your portfolio is worth $50,000, of which $10,000 (or 20%) is in the Vanguard Extended Market Portfolio, which tracks the Wilshire 4500 index of smaller-company stocks. To get your small-stock exposure up to $30,000, small-stock funds would have to account for $20,000 of the $50,000 that you have in actively managed funds. Small-stock funds thus account for 40% of your actively managed portfolio. But within your total stock fund portfolio, your small-stock exposure is limited to 30%, which is within the guidelines laid out above.

Caveat Number 1

Investment advisers often suggest that older investors make a big bet on value funds, which are renowned for their good bear market performance, while lightening up on growth funds, which can be much more volatile. Conversely, they recommend a hefty dose of growth funds for younger investors, in the hope of earning better returns.

There are three reasons why this may not be a smart strategy. First, it is not at all clear that growth and value funds live up to their reputations. Growth stocks reputedly deliver better long-term returns, but the statistical evidence doesn't necessarily support this view. Conversely, value funds are meant to perform better in bear markets. While this is generally true, it wasn't the case in the brief bear market of 1990, when value funds got hit much harder than growth funds.

Secondly, the market has gone through long periods when value was in vogue and growth out of favor. There have also been extended periods when the opposite was true. If you have made a major portfolio decision to downplay growth or value, you run the risk of missing out on the one portion of the market that just happens to be generating sizzling gains. (That danger, of course, also exists if you go overboard in buying foreign stocks, small stocks, and large-company stocks.)

Finally, you may end up with an unnecessarily volatile portfolio if you skimp on either growth funds or value funds. Because growth and value funds don't always move in sync, you can dampen the price swings in a portfolio by owning both types of funds. You will lose that benefit if you skew heavily toward growth or value.

As you grow older, a shift toward bonds and large-company stock funds and an emphasis on more sedate funds within each fund category should help to calm down your mutual fund portfolio. It is not at all clear that you will get any additional benefits by also betting heavily on value funds.

Caveat Number 2

Some mutual fund experts use a portfolio-building strategy known as style-rotation. This involves making bets, normally with a one-year to three-year time horizon, on which areas of the market will do best. If you think, for instance, that large-company growth funds will do better in the next few years than large-company value funds, then you would overweight growth and underweight value.

Savvy investors may well be able to make money using style-rotation. But it is extremely difficult to do and not an advisable strategy for most investors. Style-rotating smacks of market timing, which involves switching your money in and out of the stock market depending on whether you think stock prices will rise or fall. Market timing may seem like a prudent strategy, but there is a danger that you will misjudge the market and end up sitting on the sidelines while stocks are posting handsome gains.

Style-rotation can be equally perilous. If you start playing the style-rotation game, you may be inclined to totally ignore areas of the market that seem excessively overvalued. But the market constantly surprises investors. Segments that seem overvalued will often go on to become even more overvalued, thus defying the pundits. Similarly, areas that seem downtrodden and undervalued can stay out of favor for years. Style-rotaters, who are making shorter-term bets, can end up getting badly burned because of these market trends. Unless you happen to own a crystal ball, style-rotation can be a dangerous game—and one you ought to avoid.

14

Strategy Number 4: Finding Bargains Among Closed-end Funds

Hey you, over there. Wanna great deal? Howdya like to buy a $10 mutual fund share for just $8.50?

Sound too good to be true? It isn't. In the otherwise straightforward world of mutual funds, there is an exotic corner where investors can buy funds for a fraction of their real value. These funds are sometimes known as exchange-traded funds or publicly traded funds or closed-end funds. But whatever you want to call them, they offer the chance to add substantially to your returns.

This is probably the book's most complicated chapter. Investors who don't want to do a lot of trading, and instead are content to buy and hold a portfolio of mutual funds, can ignore what follows and move straight on to chapter 15. But if you find the market enthralling and would like the chance to further bolster your returns, read on.

How does strategy number 4 fit in with the three other strategies? Based on the previous chapters, you should have decided how to divvy up your portfolio among different types of stock funds. For instance, you might have decided to put a third of your portfolio into index funds. The other two-thirds will be divided among five actively managed stock funds, representing the five investment styles. Because you are young and unconcerned about short-term losses, you plan to aggressively allocate your portfolio among these five actively managed funds, with a lot of emphasis on small-company stocks and foreign stocks.

With strategy number 4, you might occasionally decide to substitute a closed-end fund for one of these five actively managed mutual funds. When should you do it? That takes a little explaining.

Case Closed

A no-load mutual fund has just one share price, its net asset value, which is published in the newspaper every day. This is the price you pay whether you are buying the fund or selling it. A closed-end fund, on the other hand, has two prices. Like a regular mutual fund, a closed-end fund has a net asset value, which is the per-share value of the fund's portfolio holdings. But in addition these funds also have a publicly quoted share price, which is the price you pay if you buy or sell fund shares. Often that publicly quoted price is substantially below the net asset value, thus offering you the chance to get into the fund at a bargain price. You might, for instance, have a fund with a $10 net asset value that you can buy for $8.50 a share, the equivalent of a 15% discount (which is calculated by dividing $8.50 by $10).

Not all closed-end funds sell at discounts. In fact, when closed-end funds are first offered, they are sold at a premium to their net asset value. In a quick sales drive, full-service brokers—the same folks who sell load mutual funds—will sell a limited number of shares, taking a 7% commission for their pains. After the initial public offering, the funds are closed and no more shares are sold.

Never, ever buy a closed-end fund during its initial public offering.

In the months following the initial public offering, the fund's premium tends to slowly erode, and before long the share price is trading below its net asset value, so that the fund can be bought at a discount.

There is no real trick to spotting funds trading at a discount. Most closed-end stock funds figure out their net asset values as of the close of the markets each Friday. To get that number, look at *Barron's* on Saturdays or the *New York Times* or the *Wall Street Journal* on Mondays. There you will find a listing for closed-end funds that includes four pieces of information for each: the fund's name, its net asset value, its share price, and the percentage difference between the share price and the net asset value (in other words, the premium or discount). A growing number of funds are now starting to price their portfolios every day; this information is normally available if you call a fund's toll-free telephone number.

If a fund trades at a steep discount, that is when you should consider buying. In purchasing a steeply discounted closed-end fund, you are hoping to make a twin gain. As with a regular mutual fund, you want the closed-end fund's portfolio manager to produce decent gains. But in addition you want the discount to narrow, so that you get an extra gain with the closed-end fund that you wouldn't get if you bought a regular mutual fund.

After a closed-end fund's initial public offering, you can't buy shares from the fund itself, as you would with a regular mutual fund. Instead, the only way to get into a closed-end fund is to buy some of the shares that trade on the New York Stock Exchange, the American Stock Exchange, or the Nasdaq stock quotation system. In essence, buying shares in a closed-end fund is just like buying shares in IBM or General Motors.

When buying closed-end fund shares, don't use a full-service broker, such as those employed by Merrill Lynch &

Co. or Smith Barney Shearson Inc. These brokers don't just complete transactions for investors; they also give advice. As a result, full-service brokers charge relatively high commissions.

If you want to buy a closed-end fund, use a discount broker like Fidelity Discount Brokerage, Quick & Reilly, or Charles Schwab & Co. A discount broker, like a full-service broker, will help you buy and sell shares. But there the similarities end. Discount brokerage firms aren't in the business of giving investors advice. Unlike a full-service brokerage firm, they don't employ hundreds of salesmen who are trying to persuade customers to buy and sell securities. All discount brokerage firms do is complete transactions, for which they charge relatively modest fees. Discount brokers are used by investors who know what they want to buy and sell and thus don't need a broker's advice.

Shopping at the Discount Store

How should you go about picking closed-end funds? There are three key considerations:

▪ You want funds that will play a role in your diversified fund portfolio, based on the portfolio weightings you have selected after reading chapters 11, 12, and 13. As a result, you need to figure out which of the five investment styles is used by a particular fund. The appendix, which includes some closed-end funds, should help you on that score. Many closed-end funds are highly specialized, sticking only with the stocks of a single foreign country or a single industry. You should skip these funds and buy only those that are well-diversified.

▪ You want funds that meet the same criteria as you would use in picking a regular mutual fund. As with any mutual fund, you are looking for a fund with performance consistency, modest expenses, and a fund manager with a good track record. Some of this information can be obtained by calling the fund, while other data will be contained in a fund's annual report.

• You want to buy funds that trade at a discount of 10% or more. Better-known funds, like Gabelli Equity Trust and Templeton Emerging Markets Fund, rarely sell at such big discounts. But if you are patient, this does occasionally happen. During market crashes, closed-end fund discounts often widen dramatically. This is an excellent time to switch out of regular mutual funds and into closed-end funds.

In buying closed-end funds, don't just buy the funds with the biggest discounts. You may well end up with a fund with a rotten record that deserves its lowly stock price. And don't just buy a fund because it has an excellent record. If you are not careful, you will end up buying a fund that is at a narrow discount or even at a premium.

The goal is to buy well-run closed-end funds at deep discounts that you can substitute for the no-load funds you have in your portfolio. Thus if the closed-end Royce Value Trust is trading at a 10% discount, you might choose to buy it for your portfolio instead of a regular mutual fund that buys small-company value stocks.

But it is only worth making that substitution if the discount is big enough. If you are faced with a choice between a good no-load fund and a good closed-end fund, you should always pick the no-load fund if the closed-end fund isn't at a double-digit discount. Why? The closed-end fund could fall to an even steeper discount, quickly handing you a 10% or greater loss.

When you buy a closed-end fund trading at a large discount, you are hoping both for the discount to narrow and for the fund's underlying portfolio to perform well, thus giving you a twofold gain. If the discount does narrow, consider selling and either buying another closed-end fund at a large discount or buying a regular no-load mutual fund. Why should you consider selling? The twofold gain you got—from a narrowing of the discount and from good performance of the underlying portfolio—could go into rapid reverse if there is a market correction. In that case, you could suffer a double whammy, with the discount widening and the value of the underlying portfolio tumbling.

What happens if you buy a fund at a deep discount and its shares stay stuck at their lowly level? You still gain. Imagine that you buy $850 of a closed-end fund's stock, when the underlying portfolio value was $1,000. The fund thus trades at a 15% discount. After you buy shares, the discount doesn't budge.

Don't despair. Like a regular mutual fund, the closed-end fund will probably make capital gains and income distributions each year. Suppose those distributions are equal to 10% of the portfolio's value. On a net asset value of $1,000, that 10% is the equivalent of $100. But if you paid only $850 for your shares, the payout isn't 10%, but rather 11.8% (calculated by dividing $100 by $850). Thus even if the fund's discount doesn't budge, you are still earning a superior return.

What should you do with this $100 in income and capital gains distributions? Like regular mutual funds, closed-end funds allow you to reinvest your distributions in additional fund shares. But this is worth doing only if you can reinvest the money at the current share price. If you have to reinvest at net asset value, you are better off taking your $100 distribution in cash and reinvesting it in the shares of a regular no-load mutual fund.

Why So Cheap?

A host of reasons have been offered for closed-end fund discounts. Three explanations seem particularly convincing. The first centers on the fact that closed-end funds, like regular mutual funds, charge annual expenses. These expenses are not a cost you would incur if you got hold of the fund's annual report and then bought all the stocks in the portfolio yourself. Thus the discount exists to compensate investors for the fund's annual expenses.

Here is how that works. Imagine a $100 portfolio with $1 of annual expenses that you expect to return 10% a year before expenses. After you deduct the $1 in annual expenses, the fund will earn not $10, but $9. In order for the fund to return 10% to a new buyer, it has to trade at $90, or a 10% discount. The reason: $9 divided by $90 translates into a 10% annual return, which is the rate of return you would have earned if you had simply replicated the fund's portfolio by buying each of the stocks that the fund owns.

Of course, buying all the stocks in the portfolio would be extremely troublesome and, because of portfolio changes during the year, there is no guarantee that this strategy would generate returns as good as those earned by the fund. But to some extent those considerations are also figured into closed-end fund share prices. Those funds that have good records, such as Bergstrom Capital and Source Capital, or those with portfolios that are tough to replicate, like Templeton Emerging Markets Fund, tend to trade at narrow discounts or even sizable premiums.

There is a second explanation for the persistence of discounts among closed-end funds. There is precious little information available about these funds, which tends to exacerbate the inefficiencies in the closed-end market. While numerous directories, magazine surveys, and newsletters are devoted to regular mutual funds, closed-end funds receive scant attention.

Some of the publications mentioned in chapter 3 provide coverage of closed-end funds. *Forbes* magazine includes the funds in its annual survey of mutual fund performance. Information on closed-ends is also available in Sheldon Jacobs's *Handbook for No-Load Fund Investors*. But once again, the best publication in the field, though also the most pricey, comes from Morningstar, Inc., of Chicago. *Morningstar Closed-End Funds*, which costs $195 a year, first appeared in late 1991. Because it is so new, you aren't likely to find it at many public libraries. If you plan to dabble in closed-end funds only occasionally, the *Handbook for No-Load Fund Investors* should provide you with the information you need. But if you plan to invest heavily in closed-end funds and have a relatively large portfolio, consider subscribing to Morningstar's service.

In addition to fund expenses and a lack of information, there is a third reason why discounts persist. Unlike the rest of the stock market, the buying and selling of closed-end funds is still dominated by the small investor. Professional money managers may be perfectly happy to manage the portfolio of a closed-end fund, but they are reluctant to buy closed-end funds managed by other managers. The reason: If a professional money manager buys a closed-end fund for one of his client's accounts, he is in effect charging that client two sets of fees: the fee that money managers charge for their own services, plus the annual expenses charged by the closed-end fund. (For the same reason, professional money managers are normally reluctant to invest a client's money in a regular mutual fund.)

Because professional money managers typically avoid buying closed-end funds for their clients' accounts, the buying and selling of closed-ends remains the almost exclusive preserve of the small investor. As a result, the closed-end market tends to be more inefficient than other parts of the stock market.

The Perils of Dual-Purpose Funds

There is one group of funds for which the discounts and premiums are not what they seem. These are the so-called dual-purpose funds. Only three of these funds now exist: Convertible Holdings, Gemini II, and Quest for Value Dual

Purpose Fund. Dual-purpose funds have two classes of shares outstanding, income shares and capital shares. The income shares get all the dividends kicked off by the fund's portfolio, while the capital shares benefit to the extent that there are any capital gains.

There is a basic inequity in the dual-purpose structure that benefits the income shareholders. The income shares are paid dividends each year, while the capital shareholders get nothing. Instead, all capital gains are reinvested back into the fund. These gains will be paid out to the capital shareholders when the funds liquidate, which, in the case of all three funds mentioned above, will happen in 1997. In the meantime, that growing pool of capital generates a growing stream of dividends, which gets paid to the income shareholders each year.

Given this inequity, income shares command huge premiums compared to their 1997 liquidation values, while capital shares trade at steep discounts to their current net asset value. Don't take these premiums and discounts at face value. For a further discussion of dual purpose funds, see the listing in the appendix for Gemini II.

Trading Away Your Gains

Be careful not to let brokerage commissions take too big a chunk out of your returns. Using a discount broker to buy closed-ends will certainly help. In addition, you should avoid buying closed-end fund shares in lots that are too small. If you buy only $1,000 worth of stock, you are likely to end up paying at least $35 to buy and $35 to sell, even with a discount broker. That $70 roundtrip commission, on a $1,000 trade, is the equivalent of paying a 7% sales charge.

If you are a big trader—dealing in lots of 3,000 or 4,000 shares—you should be able to cut a deal with your broker so that you can trade for, say, five cents a share. Many investors, however, just won't have the money to make trades of that magnitude. If that is the case, try to keep both your trading—and your commission costs—to a minimum.

Another way to control costs is to be careful in your buying and selling. Because fund share prices can jump around fairly sharply, if you put in an order to buy and sell at the market price, you could end up paying substantially more or less than you intended. Closed-end fund shares typically trade at around $10 a share, so that even modest price movements can make a significant difference to a fund's value. On a $10 share price, for instance, a 25-cent drop in price would cut 2.5% from your return.

When buying or selling closed-end funds, active traders often don't accept the prevailing market price. Instead, they decide on the prices at which they are willing to buy or sell, and then place limit orders that will be executed when those prices are hit. A trader might, for instance, want to sell 1,000 shares at 10⅛, but the fund's shares are currently quoted at 9⅞. By putting in a limit order that specifies sale of the shares at 10⅛, he can be assured of getting that price—providing, of course, that the fund's shares rise to 10⅛.

□PART V□
BETTING ON BOND AND MONEY MARKET FUNDS

15

Cheap Thrills: How to Select Bond and Money Market Funds

Bond funds and money market funds may be lackluster investments, but they are also firm favorites with the faint of heart. Money market funds account for 34% of mutual fund industry assets, bond funds for another 36%. Despite their superior long-term performance, stock funds finish third in the popularity rankings, with 30% of fund industry assets.

This book will, I hope, persuade you to join the minority and keep the bulk of your money in stock funds. But there is still a place for bond and money market funds in your portfolio. What role should these funds play? It helps to think about your mutual fund holdings in two parts, your long-term investment portfolio and your emergency money.

Within your investment portfolio, you should boost your bond fund holdings as you grow older. Consider lightening up on stock funds and moving into bond funds when you are 10 years away from retirement, with the aim of having roughly half your investment portfolio in bonds by the time you quit the workforce. (This issue will be addressed in greater detail in chapter 17.)

Even if you are relatively young, you may choose to hold bonds in your investment portfolio because you find it too frightening to be wholly invested in stocks. Such a strategy can carry a steep price tag, because you are likely to end up with lower long-term results. If you are more than 10 years from retirement, try to keep your bond fund holdings to a bare minimum and certainly don't let these funds grow to be more than 25% of your overall investment portfolio's value.

Whatever your age, if you plan to hold more conservative funds in your investment portfolio, lean toward bond funds rather than money market funds. Over a two- or three-year period, even the most conservative bond fund is likely to return 1.5 or 2 percentage points a year more than a money market fund.

In addition to owning bond funds within your investment portfolio, you should also use either bond or money market funds to hold some emergency money that isn't part of your long-term investment money. With emergency money, the idea is to have some cash that you can draw on should you lose your job or have an unexpectedly large medical bill or suddenly need to make a major house repair.

A money market fund or a more conservative bond fund, like an adjustable-rate mortgage fund or a short-term corporate or government bond fund, is the best place for this emergency money. Consider funds like Benham Adjustable Rate Government Securities Fund, Neuberger & Berman Limited Maturity Bond Fund, T. Rowe Price Adjustable Rate U.S. Government Fund, Vanguard Money Market Reserves–Prime Portfolio, or Vanguard Short-Term Corporate Portfolio. Don't put your emergency money in a stock fund. If you have an emergency, you could end up having to cash in your stock fund shares at a time when the stock market is in a slump.

How much emergency money should you keep? The amounts suggested are all over the lot. Investment advisers often say you should have emergency money equal to three or even six months' living expenses. Some investors don't keep any emergency money at all, figuring that in a pinch they can always run up their credit card bill or get by with some astute juggling of their checkbook.

The right amount will depend a lot on your personal situation. Is your job secure? Are you a homeowner, thus facing potentially expensive home repairs? Do you feel more comfortable knowing that you have emergency money that you can easily draw on? Whatever amount you settle on, the key is to consider this money as a pool of cash that is separate from your investment portfolio. The amount involved shouldn't be allowed to grow too big. After all, this money isn't meant to be in risky investments but, as a consequence, it is also never going to generate fabulous returns.

Whether you are investing your emergency money or buying a bond fund for your investment portfolio, there are two key dangers to avoid: buying a fund just because it boasts a lavish yield and buying a fund that levies high fees. These two dangers are discussed below.

Consider the Costs

The huge sums of money stashed away in bond and money market funds are especially perturbing when you realize how uninspiring these funds are. The fact is that there are no great money market fund managers, and star bond fund managers are rare indeed. In any one year, there is typically only the slightest difference between the best funds in any one category and the worst.

Over the five years ended December 31, 1992, for instance, the top-performing money market fund returned 7.3% a year, while the poorest performer gained 5.3% annually.

The spread between the best and worst isn't much larger if you look at the different categories of bond funds. For instance, take a look at the performance of Government National Mortgage Association bond funds (known as Ginnie Mae funds) for the five years ended December 1992. This was a favorable period for bond fund performance, with interest rates dropping. Over the five years, the best Ginnie Mae fund returned 11.6% a year. And the worst? It was up 8.7% annually, or 2.9 percentage points less than the top performer, according to Lipper Analytical Services. Over time, a difference of 2.9 percentage points a year can add up to a lot of money. But compared to the annual variations in stock fund performance, that 2.9 percentage points is minuscule.

What explains the differences in bond and money market fund performance? Unlike with actively managed stock funds, the biggest factor isn't the skill or luck of the portfolio manager. Instead, the key variable is each fund's annual expenses. The average taxable bond fund has annual expenses of around 0.93%, and the average money market fund charges 0.76%. But the most costly bond funds charge more than 2% annually, and the more expensive money market funds take 1% or more. The most efficient bond and money funds, meanwhile, charge as little as 0.25%. That doesn't mean the bond and money market funds with the lowest expenses will be the top performers in any one year. But because of their cost advantage, these funds are likely to be close to the top of the mutual fund rankings.

It is not just annual expenses that are important in picking bond funds. So, too, is the other main cost of mutual fund investing, fund sales commissions. Money market funds don't charge sales commissions, but many bond mutual funds do. Bond fund sales commissions are typically somewhat less than stock fund sales charges. Nonetheless, because long-term bond fund returns are lower than those of stock funds, bond fund investors who pay a sales charge start out with an even bigger disadvantage than stock fund investors who pay a commission. As a result, when it comes to bond fund investing, sticking with no-load funds is crucial.

Which no-load bond and money market funds have the

lowest expenses? There is no contest. If you want to invest in low-cost funds, the place to go is Vanguard Group. The Valley Forge, Pennsylvania, fund group, by virtue of its unique not-for-profit ownership structure, has minuscule expense ratios.

This ownership structure has been a bonanza for owners of Vanguard's bond and money market funds. According to Lipper Analytical Services, Vanguard Money Market Reserves–Prime Portfolio was the third-best performer for the five years ended December 1992, out of a possible 159 funds. Similarly, Vanguard's GNMA fund was a top performer in its category, ranking second out of 31 funds that have been around for the five-year period ended 1992.

Other Vanguard funds have also performed well. Vanguard's Short-Term Corporate Portfolio, for instance, was third in its category for the five-year period, and the Investment Grade Corporate Portfolio ranked as the top performer in its group.

That brings us to the first golden rule of investing in money market funds and bond funds: Try to stick with the funds with the lowest annual expenses and never, ever pay a sales commission. Invariably that will lead you to one of Vanguard's funds.

Yielding to Total Return

If you avoid load funds and instead stick with the lowest-cost bond and money market funds, you will probably do just fine. But there is an additional danger you have to watch for: buying a bond fund just because it boasts a seductively high yield.

One of the most common errors made by fund investors is to buy a fund based on yield and ignore a fund's total return, which reflects not only a fund's dividend yield but also any change in a fund's share price. With some of the more exotic bond funds, a fund's high yield may come at the expense of a fall in the fund's share price, either because the fund is taking a lot of risk or because the fund's manager is playing tricks to pump up the fund's yield.

Risk? Yield-pumping? Bear with me while I explain.

Like Baskin-Robbins ice cream, bond and money market funds come in a bewildering array of flavors. Some funds stick only with government bonds, while others also buy bonds issued by corporations. Some invest only in U.S. bonds, while others also dabble in foreign bonds. Some funds invest in bonds with a long time until maturity, while others buy securities that will be redeemed within just three months or even less.

In essence, these funds can end up taking three different risks:

- They can take credit risk, by buying bonds that are more likely to default on their interest payments.
- They can take exchange-rate risk, by investing in foreign bonds that could fall in value for U.S. holders if the dollar should rise in the foreign exchange market.
- And they can take interest-rate risk, by buying bonds with a long time until maturity. If interest rates rise, these long-term bonds will fall in value, because they are less attractive than the newer, higher-yielding bonds that are now being issued. The price of the old bonds will decline, and their yields rise, until they reach the point where their yields are in line with the current market interest rate.

For assuming any of these three risks, an investor typically is rewarded by earning a higher yield. A money market fund that buys only U.S. government securities won't make much money because it essentially takes no risk. There is no real credit risk, because the securities are issued by the U.S. government, which few people seriously imagine will default on its debt. There is no interest-rate risk, because money market funds hold securities with less than three months until maturity. Finally, there is no exchange-rate risk, because these funds are buying only U.S. dollar–denominated securities.

In fact, because money market funds are deemed to be so safe, they are allowed by the Securities and Exchange Commission to maintain a fixed share price, which is normally pegged at $1. Because of this fixed share price, there is essentially no difference between a money market fund's yield and its total return.

But with bond funds, where share prices can bounce around sharply, there can be wide divergences between yield and total return. Take, for instance, high-yield bond funds, often called junk bond funds. These funds typically yield more than any other bond funds, with good reason. While junk funds are generally buying only bonds issued by U.S. corporations, so that they aren't taking any exchange-rate risk, they are assuming some interest-rate risk and a great deal of credit risk. The reason: These funds are buying the bonds of companies that could go bankrupt and default on their interest payments.

Anybody who owns a junk bond fund should pay scant attention to yield and instead concentrate on total return. Because of bond defaults, a junk fund's share price will tend to decline over time. As a result, the fund's total return— which is the true return earned by shareholders—will be somewhat lower than the fund's annual dividend yield.

That lesson was driven home to many investors in 1989 and 1990, when the junk bond market collapsed. In those two years, junk funds continued to kick off big dividend payments even as junk fund share prices crumbled. For many inexperienced investors who didn't understand what they owned, the junk bond market's collapse was devastating. Consider the letter I received in 1990: "I am 68 years old and retired. Two-and-a-half years ago a broker invested $80,000 (my life savings) in a junk bond fund unbeknown to me. I sold it a week ago and lost $32,000. This is a terrible kick in the groin when one is 68 years old. A terrible kick at any age."

The fund industry has sometimes gone out of its way to cater to investors' lust for high-yielding funds. In the mid-1980s, for instance, government-plus funds were all the rage. These funds bolstered their dividend payouts by writing options against their government bond portfolios. By writing options, the funds earned additional money that they could pay out to shareholders. But by writing the options, the funds also gave up the potential for capital gains. As a result, the lavish dividends came at the expense of shrinking fund share prices, so that anybody who tried to live off those dividends was, in effect, consuming his own capital.

By the time some shareholders discovered this, their savings were already seriously depleted. An anguished Florida retiree sent me the following note in 1991: "My MFS Government Income Plus Trust and my wife's Putnam High-Income Government Trust—both purchased in 1987—have gotten 'whacked,' eating into their own capital. If I hold the bond funds long enough, and if interest rates go down further, will the asset value go back up some day? Is there a precedent?" Unfortunately, the share price of the two funds is unlikely to ever return to their earlier level.

The lesson: A fund that has an unusually high yield is probably taking an unusually high degree of risk, whether it is credit risk or exchange-rate risk or interest-rate risk. Alternatively, the fund could be playing games to pump up its yield. As a consequence, the fund—and your investment—may end up suffering mightily.

What should you do if a fund seems to have an inordinately high yield? The fund could boast a high yield because it has minuscule expenses, but the high yield could also result from taking excessive risk or from yield-pumping. To make sure the fund is a good buy, find out its total return for the past one, three, five, and ten years. Then compare those returns to other funds that buy similar sorts of bonds. If the high-yielding fund turns out to have a mediocre total return performance, look elsewhere.

That brings us to our second golden rule of bond fund investing: Never, ever buy a bond fund because it boasts a high current yield. Focus instead on a fund's total return.

16

A Question of Interest: Four Strategies for Bond Fund Investors

Few investors have ever gotten rich investing in bond funds. But many, it seems, have ended up disappointed. These investors thought they were making a conservative investment, but they earned miserable returns because they ignored costs and bought based on yield.

To help you earn reasonable returns with your bond fund money, four strategies are described below. The first three should deliver decent returns while allowing you to avoid a lot of hassles and nasty surprises. The fourth strategy is for more adventurous investors. It has the potential to generate higher returns, but it also involves greater complexity.

Strategy Number 1: Coming Up Short

The first strategy is the simplest and least risky: Buy a short-term corporate or government bond fund, one that owns bonds with less than five years to maturity. These short-term bond funds, such as Fidelity Short-Term Bond Portfolio, Scudder Short-Term Bond Fund, and Vanguard Short-Term Corporate Portfolio, generate far better yields than money market funds and pay out almost as much as funds that own bonds with 20 or 30 years until maturity.

But unlike with long-term bond funds, the share price of a short-term bond fund doesn't swing around much in response to interest rate changes. That is clearly a disadvantage when interest rates are falling and bond prices are rising. But it also means your portfolio is much better protected should interest rates rise and bond prices tumble. Short-term bond funds are an ideal investment for those who want to take a little bit more risk with their emergency money without going too far out on a limb.

Those in the top tax brackets may find that they are better off with a short-term municipal bond fund, like T. Rowe Price Tax-Free Short-Intermediate Fund, USAA Tax-Exempt Short-Term Fund, Vanguard Municipal Limited-Term Portfolio, and Vanguard Municipal Short-Term Portfolio. You might, for instance, get a choice between a short-term corporate bond fund paying 5% and a short-term municipal bond fund paying 4%. If you are in the 28% tax bracket, you would probably do better with the municipal bond fund. How so? Muni funds kick off income that is exempt from Federal taxes and, in some cases, from state and local taxes as well. Thus, the muni fund with its 4% yield would have a "tax equivalent" yield of 5.56% for somebody in the 28% tax bracket, which is better than the 5% yield you could get with a short-term corporate bond fund. If you phone a fund group, they should be able to give you the tax equivalent yields for their muni funds.

Investors may also want to investigate so-called single-state municipal bond funds, which pay income that is exempt from both Federal and state and local taxes, presuming you own a single-state muni fund for your state. Single-state muni funds have become wildly popular; there are now funds available for virtually every state.

But despite the additional tax savings that come with a single-state muni fund, you may want to stick with a national muni fund that buys bonds from around the country. As with regular bond funds, muni funds take varying degrees of interest-rate risk, depending on the maturities of the bonds they buy. If you are looking for a muni fund that owns shorter-maturity bonds, you will get far more choice among national muni funds. There is considerably less choice among single-state muni funds, unless you live in states like California or New York, where there are many funds available.

Strategy Number 2: Indexing

As a second strategy, you should consider using the Vanguard Bond Market Fund, a bond index fund that charges annual expenses of just 0.20%. An index fund buys many or all of the securities in a particular market index and thereby hopes to replicate the index's performance. The Vanguard Bond Market Fund seeks to track the performance of the Salomon Brothers Broad Investment-Grade Bond Index, an index fund that is comprised of roughly 70% government and government-agency bonds, with corporate bonds accounting for most of the remaining 30%.

The share price of the Vanguard Bond Market Fund is more sensitive to changing interest rates than a short-term bond fund, because the Vanguard fund owns bonds with a longer time until maturity.

Indexing the bond market has proved remarkably successful. Over the five years ended December 31, 1992, Vanguard Bond Market Fund returned 63.7%, according to Lipper Analytical Services. That makes it the third-best-performing bond fund, out of a possible 18 that also buy investment-grade bonds with a similar five- to ten-year maturity range.

Given that success, it wouldn't be surprising if the fund industry launched more of these funds.

Strategy Number 3: Gross Returns

A third strategy is to buy either Harbor Bond Fund or PIMCO Total Return Fund. What is so special about these funds? Fund manager William Gross is widely considered to be the country's best bond fund manager.

In running both the PIMCO fund and the Harbor fund, Gross invests largely in top-quality corporate or government bonds with maturities of between 5 and 15 years. This is the same territory covered by the Vanguard Bond Market Fund. Indeed, Lipper Analytical Services includes all three funds in the same fund category.

The Harbor and PIMCO funds occasionally stray beyond high-quality U.S. corporate and government bonds. For instance, the two funds can also make small investments in foreign securities and junk bonds. Over the years, Gross has astutely moved among the different parts of the bond market, generating a stellar record along the way.

With both PIMCO Total Return Fund and Harbor Bond Fund, investors can get Gross's bond-picking skills at a relatively low cost. The PIMCO fund has annual expenses of 0.42%, while Harbor Bond Fund charges 0.77% a year. But the Harbor fund demands a minimum initial investment of just $2,000, versus $500,000 for PIMCO. However, investors can get into PIMCO Total Return with a $1,000 minimum investment (and the payment of a small transaction fee) if they use the Mutual Fund Marketplace operated by Charles Schwab & Co., the discount brokerage firm. If you plan to invest with Gross for at least a couple of years, the PIMCO fund with its lower expenses is probably a better deal, even if you have to go through Schwab and pay a transaction fee.

Strategy Number 4: The Triple Play

There is a fourth strategy you may want to consider, one that is more complex but also potentially more rewarding. This strategy is probably best used by those with substantial bond portfolios, rather than by those who are simply looking for a place to park their emergency money. The idea is to split your bond portfolio equally between three funds: a government bond fund, a high-yield junk bond fund, and a foreign bond fund. The reasoning behind this mix is the same reasoning that applies when putting together a diversified stock fund portfolio. The notion is that by combining these three funds you can get superior returns with less volatility.

How does it work? Each of the three fund types faces a different sort of risk. The chief risk facing a government bond fund is interest rate risk. With a global bond fund, foreign exchange rate fluctuations are the biggest risk. And with junk bond funds, the biggest potential problem is a deterioration in the credit quality of the bond fund's portfolio.

Fears about each of these risks—interest-rate risk, exchange-rate risk, and credit risk—will loom large at certain times. Concerns about credit quality are most prominent during a recession. Concerns about rising interest rates are most prevalent when the inflation rate appears to be on the rise, which normally occurs not during a recession but when the economy is expanding rapidly. The foreign exchange markets are enormously volatile and over the short term seem entirely unpredictable. But over longer periods, exchange rates tend to reflect the differing inflation rates in different countries. Thus, while a rapid U.S. inflation rate may be bad news for government bond investors, it can be good news for foreign bond holders, because the dollar may fall in response. This will make foreign bonds more valuable for U.S. holders.

Because interest-rate, exchange-rate, and credit risks tend to worry investors at different times, a portfolio that has only partial exposure to each of the three risks will tend to be relatively calm, with one part of the portfolio surging while another part is slumping. In addition, the portfolio should generate decent returns over the long haul, because it is exposed to some of the better-performing segments of the bond market.

Vanguard Group doesn't offer a foreign bond fund, so investors may want to use Fidelity Global Bond Fund, T. Rowe Price International Bond Fund, or Scudder International Bond Fund. Vanguard offers a well-run junk bond fund with extremely low expenses. But in picking a junk bond fund, costs aren't the key criteria. Instead, you should put more emphasis on a fund's record and on the tenure of the portfolio manager, just as you would with a stock mutual fund. As a result, while you might want to use the Vanguard fund, you should also consider highly regarded junk bond funds like Fidelity Spartan High-Income Fund, T. Rowe Price High-Yield Fund, Nicholas Income Fund, and Financial Funds-High Yield Portfolio, distributed by Denver's Invesco Funds Group. None of these funds charges a sales commission.

A diversified bond fund portfolio might look something like this:

33% Vanguard Intermediate-Term U.S. Treasury Portfolio
33% T. Rowe Price International Bond Fund
33% Financial Funds-High Yield Portfolio

For those intrigued by the three-fund approach but reluctant to buy so many funds, an alternative strategy is to purchase the T. Rowe Price Spectrum Income Fund. The fund makes its money by buying seven other T. Rowe Price funds: a Ginnie Mae fund, a short-term bond fund, an equity-income fund, a junk bond fund, a foreign-bond fund, a money market fund, and a high-quality bond fund.

The T. Rowe Price Spectrum Income Fund doesn't charge a fee for its services. But investors effectively end up paying the expenses of the underlying funds. Those expenses, while reasonable, don't rival the bare-bones expense ratios offered by Vanguard Group.

Moreover, Spectrum Income, with its seven funds, follows a slightly different strategy from the three-fund approach described above. But you may still want to use the T. Rowe Price fund. Spectrum Income offers the benefits of bond market diversification while relieving you of the administrative hassle of trying to diversify by yourself.

Whichever of the above four strategies you adopt, don't expect to make big gains. Bonds are there to provide safety and income. For growth, you should look to the stock fund portion of your portfolio.

17

Investing Through the Ages: How to Change Your Portfolio as You Grow Older

The day you retire, like the day your child heads off to college, marks the beginning of the big payback. After years of saving, you can now start reaping the rewards, by tapping into the mutual fund portfolio that you have spent so many years building.

When this time rolls around, you clearly don't want to be too heavily invested in the stock market. Stock mutual funds may be a wonderful investment if you plan to stick with them for a long time. But if you need your money quickly, the stock market is a wretched place to keep your cash. The day-to-day swings in share prices, of no significance to the long-term investor, suddenly loom large if you have to cash in your portfolio next month or even next year.

That is why investors start moving out of stock funds and into bond funds as they approach retirement and face the prospect of living off their portfolio. Ditto for money that has been set aside for education. As your child approaches college age, you will want to switch out of stocks and into safer investments.

But the way you handle your child's college money and the way you manage your own retirement portfolio should be quite different. Why? Your kid's college education typically will be completed in four years. You know when you will have to start paying for college and you know when the cost will be over.

That just isn't the case with retirement. Unless you are planning a judiciously timed death, you just don't know how long your money will have to last. In any case, most people don't want to run out of money when they run out of breath. Instead, they hope to leave money to their children or their pet cause or their pet cat. You may not expect to live forever, but it sure helps to plan your finances that way.

As a result, while a child's college money should be entirely in bond funds or money market funds by the time your kid enters college, no retiree should put his or her whole portfolio into bonds. If you do that and then try to live off your bond fund dividends, your retirement portfolio will end up being seriously eroded by inflation. You could end up living to regret that you are living so long.

Migrating into Bond Funds

Whether dealing with your retirement portfolio or your child's college money, you should start moving out of stocks and into bonds at least five years ahead of when you are going to need the money. Why five years? Take a look at the history of stock market returns.

Using data from Ibbotson Associates, we can divide the period since 1926 into rolling five-year periods, beginning with the five years ended December 1930, moving on to the five years ended December 1931, and so on, finishing up with the five years ended December 1992. In all, you find that there are 63 five-year stretches during this period. Of these

63 periods, there have been seven where the Standard & Poor's 500 stock index has posted a loss—and two of those seven periods occurred in the postwar period. This suggests that if your time horizon is five years or less, there is a possibility—albeit small—that you will lose money if you are invested in the stock market.

Accordingly, when your child is five years away from college and you are five years from retirement, you should stop putting additional money into the stock market and instead direct it toward a money market fund or a bond fund.

And what about the money you already have in stocks? You are going to need your child's college money in eight lump sums, one for each of the eight semesters he or she will be at college. It would be advisable to move 25% of the portfolio—the amount earmarked to pay for the two freshman semesters—out of stocks and into bonds when your kid is five years away from college. You will need the second 25% during the sophomore year, so it makes sense to move that money five years ahead of that time—and so on for money that is tagged for the junior and senior years. If you follow this strategy, you should be wholly in bonds when your child is five years away from his last college year.

Why move money out of stocks five years ahead of the date when you will need the money? For the same reason you stop putting additional money into stocks when your kid is five years away from college: If you have a holding period of five years or less, stock market history shows that there is a modest chance that you could lose money.

With retirement it is a little different. You know you want to be, say, 50% in bonds by the time you turn 65. But because you are dealing with such a big chunk of money, you clearly don't want to move half of your portfolio into bonds on some single date five years prior to your 65th birthday. At that time, the market might be in a slump. Even if it is apparently flying high, the market might be on the verge of spurting 10% or 15% higher. Therefore it makes sense to take things slowly. One strategy would be to start moving into bonds when you are 10 years from retirement. You would move 5% of your portfolio from stocks to bonds in each of those final 10 years, with the aim of hitting the 50% mark by the time you quit the workforce.

The simplest strategy is to pick a date each year and make your 5% shift from stocks to bonds, regardless of what is going on in the market. But it could pay to show a little discretion. Thus if the market dives 15% or more from its peak, you may want to shift just 2.5% of your portfolio from stocks to bonds when the time comes for your annual transfer. You would then wait until the market recovers before moving the other 2.5%. While it is inadvisable to engage in market timing, it is prudent to show some discretion in choosing exactly when to sell out of the stock market. You may also want to use similar discretion in moving your child's college portfolio from stocks to bonds.

Investing in Retirement

For retirees, deciding how much to invest in stocks is a matter of weighing your need for income against your fear of stock market downdrafts. Over the long haul, stocks will deliver higher returns, but you will have to suffer greater gyrations in the value of your portfolio. Bonds are more likely to let you sleep at night, but they won't provide you with the superior returns that you will earn in the stock market.

The mix of stocks and bonds that you settle on will determine how well you can live in retirement. In essence, you have to earn a certain amount each year just to keep up with inflation. Whatever you earn above that level is yours to spend, happy in the knowledge that you are not dipping into your capital. Remember: The value of your portfolio must increase along with inflation during the early years of your retirement. If you spend all of your gains, your portfolio will lose its purchasing power and you could end up suffering later in retirement.

In chapter 1, it was noted that stocks have historically outpaced inflation by about 7 percentage points a year and bonds by 3 percentage points a year. Thus if you retired with a $100,000 portfolio that was wholly invested in bonds, you could spend only $3,000 in the first year of your retirement, the equivalent of 3% of $100,000. If you limited yourself to consuming just 3% of your portfolio each year, over time both the amount you could spend each year and the value of your portfolio would rise with inflation.

But if you left your money in stocks, your $100,000 would theoretically allow you to spend $7,000 in the first 12 months of your retirement, and both the income stream and the value of your portfolio would thereafter rise with inflation. But keeping a retirement portfolio entirely in stocks could turn out to be a disastrous policy. In years when the stock market nosedives, your need for spending money could cause you to cash in shares when the market is at rock bottom. The market could even enter a protracted downturn, leaving your portfolio badly bloodied for four or five years.

Most retirees should pursue a middle course, not going overboard on stocks and not retreating too much into bonds. Younger retirees—those under age 75—should consider keeping between 40% and 60% of their portfolio in stocks. With 60% in stocks, you can start your retirement with a little more than $5,000 a year in spending money for every $100,000 you have saved, with the prospect that both your spending money and your capital will stay even with inflation.

Older retirees may want to be more cautious, cutting back their stock exposure to around a quarter of their total portfolio. With such a conservatively positioned portfolio, you may end up dipping into your capital to meet your income needs.

As a retiree, think about your portfolio in three parts—stock funds, bond funds, and money market funds. Each group of funds is there to play a specific role. The stock funds are there to provide inflation-beating returns; to a more modest extent, so too are the bonds. But both sets of funds can also be used as a source of spending money. To meet your income needs, you should follow a policy of gradually selling stock and bond fund shares. The idea is to cash in some of these fund shares every six or twelve months and then move the proceeds to a money market fund. Try to limit yourself to only one or two sales a year. If you start selling fund shares more frequently than that, you can create some messy accounting problems that will come back to haunt you at tax time.

View your money market fund as a temporary parking place to keep cash that you plan to spend over the next year or so. When it comes time to replenish your money market fund, consider carefully which funds to sell. In periods when stocks are flying high, you can sell off a portion of your stock fund holdings to get some spending money. If, say, your international stock fund or your small-company growth fund has lately been on a tear, consider lightening up on those funds. But if stocks are in a slump, tap into your bond funds instead.

Funds for Your Future

Parts IV and V of this book have dealt with four main topics: why you should use stock index funds; how to invest in actively managed stock funds; how to pick among bond funds and money market funds; and when to introduce bonds into your portfolio. Now it's time to stick it all together.

In table 6 on page 151 there are three sample portfolios, for three different ages. These portfolios are for your investment money; your emergency money should be kept in a separate set of funds.

The stock index portion was pegged at 35% for the 35-year-old and the 50-year-old, and held to one-third of the 65-year-old's stock portfolio.

For the portion of each portfolio devoted to actively managed funds, the portfolio weightings were adjusted to reflect the different ages. The 35-year-old has more in international and small-company stock funds, while the 65-year-old's portfolio is tilted toward large-company stocks.

If you combine the index funds and the actively managed

Table 6

MODEL BEHAVIOR

35-year-old
25% Vanguard Index Trust-Total Stock Market Portfolio (index fund)
5% Vanguard International Equity Index Fund-European Portfolio (index fund)
5% Vanguard International Equity Index Fund-Pacific Portfolio (index fund)
11% IAI Stock Fund (large-company growth)
11% Yacktman Fund (large-company value)
10% Founders Discovery Fund (small-company growth)
10% Neuberger & Berman Genesis Fund (small-company value)
18% Babson-Stewart Ivory International Fund (international)
5% Montgomery Emerging Markets Fund (international)

50-year-old
25% Vanguard Index Trust-Total Stock Market Portfolio (index fund)
5% Vanguard International Equity Index Fund-European Portfolio (index fund)
5% Vanguard International Equity Index Fund-Pacific Portfolio (index fund)
16% Vanguard World Fund-U.S. Growth Portfolio (large-company growth)
16% Neuberger & Berman Guardian Fund (large-company value)
7% Columbia Special Fund (small-company growth)
7% Nicholas II (small-company value)
19% T. Rowe Price International Stock Fund (international)

65-year-old
14% Vanguard Index Trust-Total Stock Market Portfolio (index fund)
3% Vanguard International Equity Index Fund-European Portfolio (index fund)
3% Vanguard International Equity Index Fund-Pacific Portfolio (index fund)
13% Financial Industrial Income Fund (large-company growth)
13% Dodge & Cox Stock Fund (large-company value)
3% Strong Opportunity Fund (small-company growth)
3% Pennsylvania Mutual Fund (small-company value)
8% Scudder International Fund (international)
40% Vanguard Bond Market Fund (bonds)

funds, you find that the 35-year-old's portfolio is split between 27% small-company stocks, 40% large-company stocks, and 33% foreign stocks. The 50-year-old's portfolio isn't quite so aggressive, with 21% small stocks, 50% large stocks, and 29% foreign stocks. The 65-year-old's portfolio is even more cautious, in part because of the large investment in bonds. But in addition, the mix of stock funds is quite conservative. Some 60% of the stock fund portfolio is in large-company stocks, while small stocks account for just 17% and foreign stocks for 23%.

The actively managed funds within each portfolio were also varied, so that more aggressive funds were allocated to the 35-year-old's portfolio, with more conservative funds slated for the 65-year-old.

For the bond portion of the 65-year-old's portfolio, Vanguard Bond Market Fund was used. More committed investors may want to invest a portion of their bond portfolio in the combination of junk, foreign, and U.S. government bonds described in chapter 16.

No bond funds were used for either the 35-year-old's portfolio or the 50-year-old's portfolio. If your intention is to be a long-term investor and you have the stomach for stock market price swings, then it makes sense to minimize your bond fund holdings and instead invest almost exclusively in stock funds.

But there will be readers who find the prospect of an all-stock portfolio too frightening. In the event of a market crash, they want bonds in their portfolio to provide a financial and psychological cushion. If you fall into that camp, try to keep your bond fund holdings to a relatively modest level. At most, don't let bond funds account for more than 25% of your total portfolio's value. And don't kid yourself: These bond funds are merely there to let you sleep at night. They aren't going to do much to enhance your long-run returns.

☐PART VI☐
GETTING STARTED

18

First Steps: Easing into Mutual Funds

You have struggled your way through 17 chapters. You know what sorts of funds you want to own and in what percentages. You even have your eye on a few funds. So what the heck do you do now?

The first task is to figure out how much you have to invest right now and how much additional money you are willing to stash away every month or every three months. Starting out in mutual funds is, in many ways, a lot easier if you are young, with only a few thousand dollars to invest and the prospect of gradually buying into mutual funds for years to come. It is much tougher for those who are retired and have $200,000 or $400,000 that they want to move out of CDs or a savings account and into better-performing investments.

Start with an Index Fund

Whatever your situation, however, the first fund you might want to buy is Vanguard Index Trust–Total Stock Market

Portfolio or, if you have access to a Standard & Poor's 500 stock index fund through your employer's retirement plan, a combination of that S&P 500 fund and Vanguard Index Trust–Extended Market Portfolio. These are excellent investments for novice investors, because it is tough to go wrong with an index fund. The portfolio manager isn't going to quit and he's not going to go off the rails and start dramatically underperforming the market. Whatever the market does, that is what you will get.

The only mistakes you can make with an index fund are to throw all your money into the fund in one great wad or to panic when the market next nosedives, locking in your losses by selling your fund shares. Older investors who have never invested in stocks and finally realize they have to change their investment strategy are especially prone to these two mistakes.

If you are retired or close to retirement and have never before owned stocks, move slowly. Vanguard Total Stock Market Portfolio has a $3,000 minimum. Invest that money and then watch it for a while. You might want to split the rest of your capital between a Vanguard money market fund and one or two of the firm's bond funds.

After you have gotten used to the daily price swings in the Vanguard Total Stock Market Portfolio, move a little more money into the fund. (Vanguard doesn't allow you to make telephone switches into its index funds, unless you hold the fund in an Individual Retirement Account, so you'll have to mail in checks for the additional amounts.)

Retirees who are novice stock market investors should gradually move into the market with the aim of reaching their target stock exposure within five years. If the market tumbles 20% or more, speed up your buying. But make sure the market really has dropped 20%. A 25-cent drop in the value of your Vanguard shares may seem like a calamity if you are unused to market swings, but that sure isn't a 20% drop.

If you have large sums of money to invest, avoid buying stock funds close to the end of the year. Stock funds typically make a single set of capital gains and income distributions each year, normally in late December. Owners of stock funds have to pay taxes on those distributions, even if they have only just bought shares. As a result, if you have a large sum to invest it is better to hold off buying until early January.

Doing It on Company Time

Those who are working should think how best to combine their company's defined contribution retirement plan with their other investments. More and more companies are offering 401(k) plans, which allow you to put away money for retirement out of pre-tax dollars. These plans give you a double tax advantage: Your investments have the effect of lowering your annual tax bill, plus your money gets to grow tax-deferred until it is withdrawn. In addition, your company may match part of your contribution. Because of the tax break and any company matching, a 401(k) plan is usually the first place you should invest any money that is earmarked for retirement.

If your company's defined contribution plan doesn't allow contributions out of pre-tax dollars and there is no company matching, you may not want to put any of your own money into the plan. Instead, funnel money into an IRA. Whatever your income level, your IRA investments will grow tax-deferred. And if your income is low enough, your IRA contributions will also be tax-deductible.

Even if you aren't eligible for the IRA tax deduction, there is still a good reason to favor an IRA over your company's plan. Company-sponsored plans often offer only a limited choice of investment vehicles. Unless the plan is particularly well structured, you are unlikely to have access to either a full array of index funds or to a range of actively managed funds representing the five investment styles. By contrast, with an IRA you won't be constrained at all in picking your fund investments.

Of course, in the best of all possible worlds you will be putting money into your IRA and your company plan. But it is more likely that you will be constrained by the amount you have available to save. If that is the case, weigh carefully where you want to put your retirement money. Even if you choose to make no contributions to a company-defined contribution plan, your company may be making contributions for you. As a result, you will have to be imaginative in the way you combine your company retirement program with your other investments.

IRAs provide a way to get into funds without laying out a lot of cash. Many fund groups with regular minimums of $2,500 or $3,000 will often let you open an IRA account for just $250 or $500. IRAs are particularly useful as a back-door way into some high-minimum funds. Vanguard Trustees' Commingled Fund-International Portfolio regularly demands a $10,000 minimum, for instance, but IRA investors can get into the fund for just $500. If a fund has a prohibitively high minimum, ask what you need to open an IRA account. Often the figure will be significantly lower.

But be warned: Just because a fund has a high minimum initial investment doesn't mean it is necessarily worth buying. Conversely, there are plenty of good funds that demand paltry minimums. A few of the country's best-known mutual funds, like Nicholas Fund and the Vanguard STAR Fund, require minimum initial investments of just $500.

Doing It Automatically

Some funds, like those offered by AARP Investment Program, Babson Fund Group, Founders Funds, Gabelli & Co., Invesco Funds Group, Janus Group of Mutual Funds, Neuberger & Berman Group, T. Rowe Price Associates, Strong Funds, and Twentieth Century Investors, will waive their investment minimums if you agree to stash away $25, $50, or $100 each month. You have to sign up for an automatic investment plan, in which money is automatically deducted from your bank account on a particular day each month.

(Automatic investment plans shouldn't be confused with contractual plans, which are sold by brokers and also involve investing small amounts each month. These funds charge huge upfront sales commissions that can amount to as much as 50% of your first year's investments.)

Automatic investment plans don't just force you to save. They also put into practice the time-tested investment technique known as dollar cost averaging. Dollar cost averaging involves putting a fixed sum of money into the stock market every month, regardless of what is happening to stock prices. When the market is flying high, you end up buying fewer fund shares. When it is in the dumps, your monthly investment will purchase more fund shares. Because stock prices tend to rise over time, you should eventually end up owning fund shares that are worth considerably more than the price you paid for them.

Dollar cost averaging is a simple but very effective approach to stock market investing. For those looking to invest for the long haul, it provides a straightforward way to build wealth without fretting about the direction of the stock market. And even if you make only a small regular investment, you can eventually amass a tidy sum.

For instance, imagine that every year, starting at age 30, you put $2,000 into your Individual Retirement Account. How much would you have at age 65? If you put the money into stock mutual funds, and stocks continue to deliver 7 percentage points a year more than inflation, then the real value of your money (after adjusting for inflation) would balloon to $296,000. If you then split that money into a 60% stock–40% bond mix, that would be enough to generate an income of almost $16,000 a year, in today's dollars, to enjoy through your retirement. (For contrast, imagine you put your $2,000 a year into bonds. If you earned only 3 percentage points a year more than inflation, your portfolio at age 65 would be worth just $125,000 in today's dollars.)

How much should you be saving every month? Take a look at table 7 (see page 161) and decide for yourself. The table shows the sort of returns you can expect if you invest $100 a month over certain time periods. The returns are given for three investment options: an all-stock portfolio that returned 7% a year above inflation, an all-bond portfolio that returned 3%, and a balanced portfolio of 50% stocks and 50% bonds that returned 5% a year.

First pick your investment option and the number of years you have to save. Then look at the end result you would have from saving $100 a month. If you can save only $50 every month, halve the final amount. If you can stash away $200 each month, double the final result.

There are no guarantees that in the future stocks and bonds will generate their historical average returns. Over one or two years, stock and bond market returns are entirely unpredictable. The historical averages are more likely to prevail over periods of 15 or 20 years. But even over these long stretches, your returns could well be somewhat lower or somewhat higher than those indicated in table 7.

Doing the Taxes

This is intended to be an investment book, not a book on taxation. Nonetheless no book on mutual funds would be complete without some discussion of taxes. What follows is a brief description of some of the tax issues involved in mutual fund investing. To find out more, you might try reading one of the guides to mutual fund taxation, such as those put out by Fidelity Investments and Vanguard Group.

As you build your portfolio, it is important to keep track of the paperwork you will need to calculate your taxes. Mutual funds will send you a statement every time you do a transaction. In addition, they will normally send you a statement at the end of every year and every time the fund declares a capital gains or income distribution. With money market funds and bond funds that declare monthly dividends, you can end up receiving a statement every month.

Table 7

MAKING MONEY GROW

Shown below are the year-end values you would earn by investing $100 every month, presuming you got the specified rate of return. The rates of return used—3% for bonds, 5% for a balanced portfolio, and 7% for stocks—are so-called real rates of return, which means they are the returns you would earn over and above the inflation rate. Thus the table provides an idea of how much your money will be worth in today's dollars. The figures shown here reflect historical long-term averages. From year to year, however, stock and bond returns can fluctuate enormously. Moreover, long-term future returns may vary from the historical averages. As a result, the numbers below should be used only as a rough guide to future returns.

Year	Bond Portfolio (3% annual return)	Balanced Portfolio (5% annual return)	Stock Portfolio (7% annual return)
5	$6,659	$7,141	$7,660
10	14,393	16,305	18,520
15	23,378	28,065	33,915
20	33,815	43,159	55,739
25	45,939	62,529	86,678
30	60,022	87,387	130,537
35	76,381	119,290	192,713
40	95,384	160,232	280,855

Source: T. Rowe Price Associates

Unless you hold a fund in a tax-deferred account, you will have to pay taxes on all these income and capital gains distributions.

To avoid getting snowed under by this blizzard of paper, prune your pile of portfolio statements as you go along. At year-end, fund groups will normally send you a statement listing all your transactions for the prior 12 months. If that is the case, keep that statement and throw out all the statements you received earlier in the year.

If you sell a fund, you will need all those year-end tax statements. When tax filing season rolls around, you have to calculate the cost basis for the funds you sold during the prior year. This isn't an issue with a money market fund. Because money market funds maintain a stable $1 share price, you will never have a capital gain or loss.

Unfortunately that is not the case with bond and stock funds. For these funds, to figure out your capital gain or loss you have to compare the amount you have invested in the fund with the amount you received when you cashed in your fund shares. But the amount you invested isn't simply the sum of your initial investment plus any subsequent investments. In figuring out your cost basis for tax purposes, you also have to include any capital gains and income distributions that you reinvested in additional fund shares.

One of the most common mistakes made by fund investors is to forget about these distributions. If investors simply compare the amount they invested with the amount they eventually redeemed, they end up paying tax on the entire difference, thus handing the IRS a modest bonanza.

If you add together four items—initial investment, subsequent investments, capital gains distributions that you have reinvested, and income distributions that you have reinvested—you will have the cost basis. Now subtract this figure from the amount you received when you sold your fund shares. If the resulting number is positive, you have a capital gain and will have to pay taxes on the amount involved. If it is negative, you have a loss and can use this loss to set against capital gains you might have and, to a limited extent, against income as well.

Here's an example of how this might work. Imagine you made the following transactions:

Date	Description of Transaction	Amount	Share Price	Shares Purchased (or Sold)
Jan. 1990	Initial purchase	$1,000	$12.50	80
Dec. 1990	Income distribution	48	12	4
	Cap. gain distribution	72	12	6
Oct. 1991	Purchase	750	15	50
Dec. 1991	Income distribution	62	15.50	4
	Cap. gain distribution	93	15.50	6
Jan. 1992	Redemption	(2,400)	16	(150)

For the January 1992 sale, your cost basis would be $2,025, which you get by combining your initial $1,000 purchase, the two income distributions, the two capital gains distributions, and the subsequent $750 purchase. Your capital gain for tax purposes would therefore be $375, which is calculated by deducting $2,025 from the proceeds of the sale, $2,400. (In filling out your tax return, you would have to divide the $375 into short-term and long-term capital gains.) As an investor, you actually made substantially more than $375. If you include the $275 in income and capital gains distributions that you had earlier received and paid taxes on, your total gain would have been $650. In the above example, these distributions were reinvested, thereby purchasing 20 additional fund shares.

If you sell a fund, try to sell the whole thing in one fell swoop. If you start selling funds in dribs and drabs, the tax accounting gets even more complicated. If you cash in only part of your fund holdings, you can use a couple of different methods to calculate your cost basis. For instance, the IRS will allow you to specify the shares you are selling and then use the cost basis of those shares in deciding whether you have a gain or loss. This is clearly the most tax-efficient method, because you can specify that you sold the highest cost shares, thereby minimizing your capital gain. But the IRS has stiff criteria for using this method. Unless you have a vast portfolio and a dedicated accountant, don't even think about it.

Two other methods are somewhat simpler: the average-cost method and the first-in, first-out method. The first-in, first-out method involves presuming that the first shares you bought are the ones that you sold. If you sell half your fund shares, for instance, you would have to look back through your fund statements to see how much you paid for those shares. This method typically generates the highest tax bills. Because fund share prices tend to rise over time, the shares that you have held the longest will often have the lowest cost basis.

In the example above, if you sold half your shares you would be selling 75 shares, which at $16 a share would generate a sales proceed of $1,200. Using the first-in, first-out method, you would be selling shares that you bought with your initial $1,000 purchase, at $12.50 a share. Thus your cost basis would be $937.50, the equivalent of 75 shares multiplied by $12.50 a share. Your taxable gain would be $262.50 (a number arrived at by subtracting $937.50 from $1,200).

The average-cost method is usually more tax-efficient than the first-in, first-out method. Under the average-cost method, you figure out the cost basis for your entire mutual fund holding on a per-share basis. Then, depending on how many shares you sold, you simply calculate the corresponding cost.

In the example above, for instance, you would take your total cost—$2,025—and divide it by 150 shares, for an average cost of $13.50 a share. If you sold half your shares for

$1,200, your cost basis would be $1,012.50 (calculated by multiplying 75 shares by $13.50). Your taxable gain would thus be $187.50—less than the $262.50 gain you got with the first-in, first-out method.

The average-cost method won't be as tax-efficient as the first method described, where you specify which shares you are selling. But the average-cost method is relatively simple, a major point in its favor.

Keeping an Eye on the Prize

You have your portfolio in place. You are investing regularly. You are keeping your fund statements in good order. Is there anything more you have to do?

Not much is the answer. There are a few checks you should make each year, to safeguard against any possible problems at the funds you own. For the actively managed funds that you hold, call once a year to make sure the portfolio manager hasn't retired or quit. If the old manager has disappeared, see if the new manager has a record of his or her own from running another mutual fund or from managing private accounts. If you don't get a satisfactory answer, sell. There are plenty of good funds around, so there is no reason to stick with a fund about which you have any doubts.

You should also keep an eye on each fund's performance. Consider dumping those that have lagged behind comparable funds for three or more years.

Finally, watch out for funds that try to boost expenses. This has become an unfortunate trend in the mutual fund industry. Every year a fistful of fund groups send out incomprehensible proxy statements detailing proposed fee increases. For reasons unknown, fund shareholders have voted for these increases time and again. If your fund boosts expenses to an unconscionable level, vote with your feet by selling your shares.

19

Final Thoughts: Patience, Humility, Discipline, and Making Money

If you read enough newspapers, watch enough television, and attend enough cocktail parties, you are likely to hear all kinds of investment advice, much of which sounds clichéd. But even clichés sometimes contain a grain of truth. Here are a few thoughts to consider as you venture into mutual funds.

Get time on your side. The younger you are when you start investing in the stock market, the greater your chance for earning spectacular returns. With stock market investing, being smart helps. But being young is far more important.

At any one time, there are always a dozen good reasons why you shouldn't invest in the stock market. Stock prices are too high, some will say. The market is about to tumble, others will declare. If you listen to all these pronouncements, you will never get started in the stock market.

As soon as you invest in a stock mutual fund, the stock market will go down. It always seems to happen that way.

You buy a stock fund and then you are immediately made to regret it. That is why dollar cost averaging is so useful. If you are investing on a regular basis, what happens tomorrow seems immaterial.

Your first bear market will be the worst. The ride down seems interminable. The hand-wringing and declarations of doom by the pundits are almost incessant. It will seem that there are a thousand reasons why the stock market will keep going down. Months after the market has started to rebound, these reasons will continue to be bandied around. Those who listen will miss the rally.

There will be a bear market in the next few years. Stock prices will fall maybe 20%, maybe 40%. But a bear market will indeed happen. There will be a lot of breast-beating and cries of despair. And then the market will recover and go higher.

At some point, you will become absolutely convinced that the market is heading into the tank. You will be tempted to sell all or part of your stock fund holdings and move the money into a bond fund or a money market fund. You might even do it. In all likelihood, you will end up regretting your attempt at market timing, and if you are wise, you will never do it again.

A time will come when you think one of your stock funds, representing one of the five investment styles, is destined to plunge in price because the fund's particular market sector is so overvalued. You will seriously consider selling the fund. You may indeed dump the fund. As with any attempt at market timing, you will probably end up regretting this decision.

Rules for the Game

A successful investor needs to develop an investment plan and stick with it. Here are some of the rules that you should remember:

○ Invest as much in stocks as you possibly can.

○ Aim to put together a diversified stock fund portfolio, by buying both index funds and actively managed funds.

○ Consider indexing between 30% and 50% of your stock fund portfolio. Make sure you index both the whole U.S. market and foreign markets.

○ Among actively managed funds, make sure you own at least five stock funds representing each of the five different investment styles: small-company growth, small-company value, large-company growth, large-company value, and international.

○ Establish target portfolio weightings for each of the five investment styles. At the end of every year, figure out what percentage of your stock fund portfolio is invested in each of the funds you own. Then use additional investments over the next 12 months to get your portfolio weightings back to the target percentages.

○ Avoid buying funds that don't fit into a diversified portfolio. In particular, don't buy asset allocation, balanced, sector, and global funds. Remember: Global funds include U.S. and foreign stocks, while international funds invest exclusively abroad, so you get pure foreign stock exposure only with an international fund.

○ Avoid buying too many funds; only investors with large portfolios should own more than a dozen funds.

○ Watch costs carefully. Be leery of stock funds that levy a sales commission, that have annual turnover above 200%, and that charge annual expenses of more than 1.5%. With international stock funds and small-company stock funds, be leery of those with expenses that exceed 2%.

○ Favor stock funds with strong five-year results, but don't rule out funds with shorter track records.

○ Check a stock fund's year-by-year performance record. Avoid those funds whose long-term records are built on just one or two years of fabulous performance.

- Make sure the fund manager responsible for a fund's record hasn't jumped ship.
- Be leery of small-company stock funds with more than $300 million in assets and large-company stock funds with more than $3 billion in assets.
- Never buy a closed-end fund unless it is at a discount of at least 10%, and always sell if it moves to a slight discount or a premium. When buying closed-end funds, be careful not to let trading costs wipe out your returns.
- With your retirement portfolio, start moving into bond funds when you are ten years from retirement, but don't abandon stock funds entirely. With your child's college money, begin the move to bonds when your child is five years from college.
- If you keep a pool of emergency money, use a money market fund, a short-term bond fund, or an adjustable rate mortgage fund. Never use a stock fund.
- With bond funds, never pay a sales commission and always try to invest in the funds with the lowest expenses.
- Never buy a bond fund based on its yield; instead, base your fund selection on each fund's total return.
- Make full use of your IRA and your company's 401(k) plan or profit-sharing plan.
- Use dollar cost averaging.

This book has tried to get you to think less about individual funds and more about portfolios of funds. In putting together a portfolio, you first have to decide how you want to allocate your portfolio between stock and bond funds. You next have to decide what types of stock funds you want to own and in what sorts of quantities. And only then should you start to think about which individual funds you should buy.

Keep in mind that what really counts is the performance of your portfolio. Within your portfolio, one or two funds may be getting massacred at any one time. If you start to get unnerved by that, sit down and calculate what has happened to the value of your portfolio. In all likelihood, you will find that the massacred funds have put only a modest dent in your portfolio's overall value.

There are all kinds of foolish investment mistakes and all kinds of perfectly sensible people who end up making them. You will no doubt make at least a couple of blunders. To minimize these mistakes, try to develop three qualities as an investor: discipline, patience, and humility. Discipline—to stick with your investment plan. Patience—to wait for the results. And humility—to realize that there are a lot of smart folks playing the investment game and that your best bet is to simply buy and hold a diversified portfolio of mutual funds and thereby harness the wealth-building power of the stock market.

Appendix

Figuring out a fund's investment style is one of the toughest parts of mutual fund investing. To help you get started, the funds here have been divided up based on their investment styles. There are seven categories below: large-company growth funds, large-company value funds, small-company growth funds, small-company value funds, international funds, stock index funds, and bond funds.

Growth fund managers have a tendency to prefer smaller stocks, while value managers often lean toward larger, more established companies. As a result, in the listing below you will find more small-company growth funds than small-company value funds, and more large-company value funds than large-company growth funds.

The list is not intended to be comprehensive. Instead, the principal aim of this appendix is to provide you with a starting point in your search for top-performing stock and bond funds. Many of the funds included here have stellar track records. Others are up-and-coming funds that could turn into star performers.

Also included here are the most popular no-load and low-load stock funds, those with $2.5 billion or more in assets at year-end 1992 that are still open to new investors. These funds are listed because many readers of this book will either own these funds or have heard about them. You may want to avoid these funds because of their size. In addition, some of these funds charge a sales commission.

A number of closed-end funds are listed here. These funds may be of interest if their publicly traded shares are selling at a double-digit discount to the fund's net asset value.

The statistical information below was drawn primarily from Morningstar, Inc. In addition, some of the performance data was supplied by Lipper Analytical Services. Please note that the investment minimum for each fund is often lower for IRA investments, and Uniform Gifts or Transfers to Minors Act accounts. With the exception of Fidelity Magellan Fund, the Fidelity funds listed below will waive their sales charges, providing you buy the fund in a retirement account. Closed-end funds have no fixed minimum investment; the size of an initial investment will depend upon how many publicly traded shares are purchased.

Large-company Growth Funds

Bergstrom Capital Corp.

A closed-end fund, growth-oriented Bergstrom Capital was a fabulous performer through the 1980s, soaring 525.4%, better than any other closed-end fund. But the fund has recently become a victim of its own success. One of Bergstrom Capital's long-time stock positions, Amgen, Inc., the top-flight biotechnology firm, has posted such spectacular gains that it has come to dominate the portfolio, accounting for roughly a third of the fund's assets. Fund manager Erik Bergstrom has been selling some Amgen shares. But until the Amgen stake is severely cut, this fund's results will be driven by Amgen's stock market performance, for better or worse.

Expenses: 0.88%. *Turnover:* 17%. *Stock exchange:* AMEX. *Ticker symbol:* BEM. *Telephone:* 206-623-7302.

Dreyfus Fund

Aided by a combination of skillful investment management and skillful advertising, Dreyfus Fund was the fund industry's preeminent mutual fund in the 1960s. More recently the fund's returns have been less impressive. The fund leans toward moderately priced blue-chip stocks with steady earnings growth, and it tends to keep a fair amount of assets in cash. For those seeking modest but steady gains, this fund is a reasonably good investment. But most investors would probably do better elsewhere.

Load: None. *Expenses:* 0.78%. *Turnover:* 80%. *Minimum investment:* $2,500. *Telephone:* 718-895-1206/800-645-6561.

Fidelity Magellan Fund

Magellan is the country's largest stock mutual fund, and also the one with the best 15-year record. But the record was put together by renowned stock-picker Peter Lynch, who retired in May 1990. His successor, Morris Smith, put together good performance numbers during a two-year stint at the fund. But Smith quit Magellan to take his family to Israel. Since June 1992, the fund has been run by Jeffrey Vinik, probably Fidelity's brightest stock-picker. Vinik will need all the skill he can muster. Because of its size, Magellan is an unwieldy beast. If Vinik does an exceptional job, the fund may go on beating the market. But investors are kidding themselves if they think Magellan will rank as one of the top-performing mutual funds in the years ahead.

Load: 3%. *Expenses:* 0.99%. *Turnover:* 188%. *Minimum investment:* $2,500. *Telephone:* 800-544-8888.

Financial Industrial Income Fund

This Denver-based fund is typically classified as an equity-income fund, which would usually indicate that it uses a value approach to stock-picking. But fund managers John Kaweske, Ron Lout, and Charles Mayer skip the usual value stocks, instead buying fast-growing companies that pay low dividends. To boost the fund's dividend yield, they look to an assortment of bonds, utilities, and convertible securities. For conservative investors looking for a growth-stock fund, Financial Industrial Income Fund is an excellent choice.

Load: None. *Expenses:* 0.98%. *Turnover:* 119%. *Minimum investment:* $1,000. *Telephone:* 303-930-6300/800-525-8085.

Gabelli Growth Fund

Elizabeth Bramwell isn't nearly as well known as her boss, star stock-picker Mario Gabelli. But under her stewardship, Gabelli Growth has easily outpaced both the Standard & Poor's 500 stock index and the funds managed by Mario Gabelli. She looks for earnings growth, and she will take it wherever she can find it, whether it's large corporations or small companies, prosaic industries or high-flying biotechnology stocks.

Load: None. *Expenses:* 1.35%. *Turnover:* 50%. *Minimum investment:* $1,000. *Telephone:* 800-422-3554.

General American Investors

This is a closed-end fund. A concentrated portfolio of companies with annual earnings growth of at least 15% makes General American a sizzling performer when growth stocks are doing well. It was one of the better-performing diversified closed-end stock funds during the 1980s, though the fund still lagged behind the Standard & Poor's 500 stock index. The current fund manager, William Gedale, took over the fund's management in 1989.

Expenses: 1.02%. *Turnover:* 21%. *Stock exchange:* NYSE. *Ticker symbol:* GAM. *Telephone:* 212-916-8400.

IAI Stock Fund

Julian "Bing" Carlin, who has posted knockout returns with IAI Regional Fund (see below), took over the management of IAI Stock in early 1991. Carlin started his career as a stockbroker with PaineWebber and turned his hand to portfolio management only at age 39. He puts a lot of weight on finding companies with good management, and he is rigorous about selling stocks when a company's earnings or sales growth show signs of slipping.

Load: None. *Expenses:* 1.25%. *Turnover:* 210%. *Minimum investment:* $5,000. *Telephone:* 612-376-2600/800-945-3863.

Janus Fund

Fund experts who know Janus Fund's manager James Craig say he has superb stock market instincts. Craig took over responsibility for the fund in 1986, and he has managed to outpace the Standard & Poor's 500 stock index in virtually every year since then. Janus Fund, and the other Janus Group funds, have been exploding in size since early 1989. Other fund groups have stumbled badly when faced with a similar flood of money. But so far rapid growth has done nothing to slow Janus Fund's performance.

Load: None. *Expenses:* 0.97%. *Turnover:* 152%. *Minimum investment:* $1,000. *Telephone:* 800-525-8983.

Jundt Growth Fund

A closed-end fund with impeccably awful timing, this growth-stock fund was launched in late 1991, just before growth stocks went out of favor and value investors returned to the limelight. But in the longer term this fund has two points in its favor. First, the fund is run by James Jundt, one of the most celebrated of the Minneapolis growth-stock pickers. Second, every year the fund will consider making a tender offer for its own shares, which should help to keep the discount narrow.

Expenses: 1.37%. *Turnover:* N.A. *Stock exchange:* NYSE. *Ticker symbol:* JF. *Telephone:* 612-541-0677/800-543-6217.

Tri-Continental Corp.

A closed-end fund launched in 1929, Tri-Continental emphasizes good-quality companies with sustainable earnings growth. Fund manager James Crawford, who has been running the fund since 1989, tends to stick with some of the less-pricey growth stocks. For closed-end fund buyers who want a more conservative growth-stock fund, Tri-Continental should prove more palatable than high-octane alternatives like Bergstrom Capital and Jundt Growth Fund.

Expenses: 0.68%. *Turnover:* 49%. *Stock exchange:* NYSE. *Ticker symbol:* TY. *Telephone:* 212-432-4100/800-221-2450.

Twentieth Century Growth Investors
Twentieth Century Heritage Investors
Twentieth Century Select Investors

Twentieth Century's stock funds all use a pedal-to-the-metal growth-stock style. But there are subtle differences between the funds. Twentieth Century Heritage and Twentieth Century Select invest exclusively in dividend-paying companies, so they tend to be more staid than the other Twentieth Century funds. Heritage is just a fraction of the size of Select, so it is both more nimble and also better placed to invest in both large and medium-sized companies. Thus for those looking for a moderately aggressive growth fund, Heritage is a better bet than Select, providing you don't mind suffering the price gyrations associated with the somewhat smaller stocks. Twentieth Century Growth, on the other hand, isn't restricted to dividend-paying stocks, so the fund can turn in explosive returns when the stock market is soaring. As with the three Twentieth Century funds listed below in the small-company growth section, Twentieth Century Growth should be bought only by those with a well-developed tolerance for volatility. With the exception of Twentieth Century Giftrust Investors, all Twentieth Century funds have no specified investment minimum. Shareholders, however, must automatically invest at least $25 a month if their account balance is below $1,000.

Twentieth Century Growth Investors—*Load:* None. *Ex-*

penses: 1.00%. *Turnover:* 53%. *Minimum investment:* None. *Telephone:* 816-531-5575/800-345-2021.

Twentieth Century Heritage Investors—*Load:* None. *Expenses:* 1.00%. *Turnover:* 119%. *Minimum investment:* None. *Telephone:* 816-531-5575/800-345-2021.

Twentieth Century Select Investors—*Load:* None. *Expenses:* 1.00%. *Turnover:* 95%. *Minimum investment:* None. *Telephone:* 816-531-5575/800-345-2021.

Vanguard World Fund–U.S. Growth Portfolio

Fund manager J. Parker Hall looks for companies with a record of superior earnings growth that rank as leaders within their industry sector. That strategy, which leads the fund to buy top-quality blue-chip stocks, has worked extremely well in the recent growth-stock bull market. With its slow turnover and low expenses, this fund should appeal to investors looking for a well-run growth fund that doesn't take too many risks.

Load: None. *Expenses:* 0.49%. *Turnover:* 24%. *Minimum investment:* $3,000. *Telephone:* 215-669-1000/800-662-7447.

Warburg Pincus Capital Appreciation Fund

Fund manager Andrew Massie made his mark as manager of Scudder Capital Growth Fund. But in 1989, he quit to take over Warburg Pincus Capital Appreciation, where he continues to look for medium-sized growth stocks that have fallen out of favor. Though Massie's investment style hasn't worked quite so well in recent years, his long-term record suggests that the fund's shareholders should be handsomely rewarded over the long haul.

Load: None. *Expenses:* 1.02%. *Turnover:* 56%. *Minimum investment:* $2,500. *Telephone:* 212-878-0600/800-888-6878.

Large-company Value Funds

Babson Value Fund

Many value funds spice up their portfolio with a few growth stocks, hoping to bolster their returns should value stocks languish. That sure isn't the strategy at Babson Value Fund. Managed by Roland "Nick" Whitridge, the fund owns a lot of dirt-cheap beaten-up stocks that other investors will—hopefully—one day rediscover. The fund's small size, low portfolio turnover, and reasonable expenses make it an intriguing buy. And while the fund's track record hasn't been great, Babson Value will likely sparkle if value investing returns to favor for a protracted period.

Load: None. *Expenses:* 1.01%. *Turnover:* 17%. *Minimum investment:* $1,000. *Telephone:* 816-471-5200/800-422-2766.

Dodge & Cox Stock Fund

Though this fund is registered in most of the large states, it isn't available everywhere. That's a shame. Dodge & Cox's willingness to buy and hold undervalued stocks with good long-term earnings growth potential helped the fund post the fund industry's 35th-best record for the 1980s. Dodge & Cox is run by a team of portfolio managers, so it isn't vulnerable to the departure of a star manager.

Load: None. *Expenses:* 0.64%. *Turnover:* 7%. *Minimum investment:* $2,500. *Telephone:* 415-434-0311.

Fidelity Equity-Income Fund

Manager Beth Terrana, who made her name as manager of Fidelity Growth & Income Portfolio, took over this fund in September 1990. At the time, performance was suffering mightily and investors were fleeing. Terrana—and 1991's rebounding stock market—helped turn that around. But despite Terrana's obvious talents, the fund's sales commission and huge size suggest that investors may be better off elsewhere.

Load: 2%. *Expenses:* 0.67%. *Turnover:* 97%. *Minimum investment:* $2,500. *Telephone:* 800-544-8888.

Fidelity Growth & Income Portfolio

This fund seems to be a proving ground for Fidelity's best and brightest. Both Fidelity Magellan's Jeff Vinik and Fidelity Equity-Income's Beth Terrana have had stints running this fund. These days, responsibility for the fund falls to Steven Kaye, who earlier had a good run as manager of Fidelity Blue Chip Growth Fund. As with Fidelity Equity-Income, this fund has two strikes against it—its size and its sales charge.

Load: 2%. *Expenses:* 0.86%. *Turnover:* 221%. *Minimum investment:* $2,500. *Telephone:* 800-544-8888.

Fidelity Puritan Fund

Some fund research firms classify Fidelity Puritan as a balanced fund, because it owns a mix of stocks and bonds. But Puritan's manager Richard Fentin, who has run the fund since 1987, will keep as much as 80% of the fund's portfolio in stocks, which is much higher than most balanced funds. Those already in this fund should continue to get decent results. But if you are out shopping for a conservative value fund, you will probably do better elsewhere.

Load: None. *Expenses:* 0.64%. *Turnover:* 102%. *Minimum investment:* $2,500. *Telephone:* 800-544-8888.

Gabelli Asset Fund

Managed by Mario Gabelli since its 1986 launch, Gabelli Asset Fund was a stellar performer in 1987 and 1988. But over the three years that followed, this value-oriented fund lagged badly as growth stocks roared ahead. That underperformance raised concerns about whether Mario Gabelli's money management operation had become too large for one person to handle. At this stage, the jury is still out.

Load: None. *Expenses:* 1.31%. *Turnover:* 14%. *Minimum investment:* $1,000. *Telephone:* 800-422-3554.

Gabelli Equity Trust

This is a closed-end fund. Like Gabelli Asset Fund, Gabelli Equity Trust is run by Mario Gabelli, one of the star value managers of the 1980s. Gabelli looks for stocks that are cheap compared to their so-called private market values, which is the value that a rational businessman would pay for the company. In determining a company's private market value, Gabelli puts a lot of weight on a company's free cash flow. As a result, he typically owns stocks that are quite different from those owned by more traditional value players, who emphasize stocks that are cheap relative to their earnings or book value.

Expenses: 1.26%. *Turnover:* 11%. *Stock exchange:* NYSE. *Ticker symbol:* GAB. *Telephone:* 800-422-3554.

Gemini II

A closed-end fund, Gemini II is the only way to invest with star stock-picker John Neff, who is best known as manager of Vanguard's Windsor Fund, a regular mutual fund that is now closed to new investors. Those who buy Gemini II will have to suffer some added complexity, because Gemini II is a peculiar breed of closed-end fund known as a dual-purpose fund. These funds have two classes of shares outstanding, income shares and capital shares. The income shares get all the income kicked off by the portfolio, while the capital shares benefit to the extent that there are any capital gains. Because of this peculiar division of rewards, the published discounts and premiums shown for each class of shares are meaningless.

By having two classes of shares, dual-purpose funds hope to appeal to income-oriented investors, who would buy the income shares, and more aggressive investors, who would buy the capital shares. But instead of sticking with just the income shares or just the capital shares, those interested in investing with Neff should consider buying equal quantities of both classes of shares. That way, you will get the sort of returns you would get if you bought Windsor Fund. To find out whether Gemini II's combined shares are trading at a premium or discount, add together the share price of the income and capital shares, and then compare that figure to the combined net asset value for the two classes of shares. Thus if the newspapers report that Gemini II's income shares have a published net asset value of $9.30 and the capital shares have a net asset value of $18.50, the combined net asset value would be $27.80. Now imagine that the publicly traded income shares are at $12.50 and the capital shares are at $13.25. The fund's combined stock price is thus $25.75—or 7.4% less than the fund's combined net asset value. Even at a modest discount, Gemini II could turn out to be a good investment, because the fund will liquidate in 1997, at which point shareholders will get back the fund's full net asset value.

Expenses: 0.51%. *Turnover:* 52%. *Stock exchange:* NYSE. *Ticker symbol for capital shares:* GMI. *Ticker symbol for income shares:* GMIpr. *Telephone:* 215-669-1000/800-662-7447.

Lindner Dividend Fund
Lindner Fund

Robert Lange, Larry Callahan, and Eric Ryback jointly run Lindner Fund, while Ryback has sole responsibility for Lindner Dividend Fund. Lindner Fund looks for low-debt companies that are cheap relative to earnings. Because the fund's valuation criteria are so strict, Lange, Callahan, and Ryback have taken to scouring foreign markets in their search for undervalued stocks; foreign companies now account for one-fifth of the fund's assets. Lindner Dividend Fund, meanwhile, is one of the more unusual funds geared toward high-dividend-yielding securities. To maintain the fund's high dividend, Ryback buys an assortment of junk bonds, convertible securities, and severely beaten-up stocks. Lindner Dividend is closed to new investors in early 1993, but the closing is likely to be short-lived.

Lindner Dividend Fund—*Load:* None, though 2% redemption fee on shares sold within 60 days of purchase. *Expenses:* 0.80%. *Turnover:* 24%. *Minimum investment:* $2,000. *Telephone:* 314-727-5305.

Lindner Fund—*Load:* None, though 2% redemption fee on shares sold within 60 days of purchase. *Expenses:* 0.80%. *Turnover:* 11%. *Minimum investment:* $2,000. *Telephone:* 314-727-5305.

Mutual Beacon Fund

Though not quite in a league with Fidelity Magellan Fund, Mutual Shares Fund is one of the fund industry's all-stars. The fund was the fourth-best performer in the 1970s and the 41st-best performer in the 1980s. That stellar performance attracted a flood of new cash, prompting fund manager Michael Price to close both Mutual Shares and another fund, Mutual Qualified Fund, to new investors. But there's a third fund in the group, Mutual Beacon, that is still accepting money from new investors. All three funds have similar portfolios, which include a mix of undervalued stocks and bankrupt bonds. Take care in analyzing Mutual Beacon's record. Michael Price took over the fund's management in 1985; prior to that, Mutual Beacon was run by another investment advisory firm.

Load: None. *Expenses:* 0.85%. *Turnover:* 57%. *Minimum investment:* $5,000. *Telephone:* 201-912-2100/800-448-3863.

Neuberger & Berman Guardian Fund
Neuberger & Berman Manhattan Fund
Neuberger & Berman Partners Fund

Founded by legendary value investor Roy Neuberger, Neuberger & Berman has a solid reputation as one of the fund industry's most respected value houses. While its three large-company funds rarely sizzle, the funds don't disappoint, either. Neuberger & Berman Manhattan is the most aggressive of the three funds, while Neuberger & Berman Guardian is the most conservative. Both Manhattan and Partners have had fund manager changes in the past few years.

Neuberger & Berman Guardian Fund—*Load:* None. *Expenses:* 0.82%. *Turnover:* 41%. *Minimum investment:* $1,000. *Telephone:* 212-476-8800/800-877-9700.

Neuberger & Berman Manhattan Fund—*Load:* None. *Expenses:* 1.07%. *Turnover:* 83%. *Minimum investment:* $1,000. *Telephone:* 212-476-8800/800-877-9700.

Neuberger & Berman Partners Fund—*Load:* None. *Expenses:* 0.86%. *Turnover:* 97%. *Minimum investment:* $1,000. *Telephone:* 212-476-8800/800-877-9700.

Nicholas Fund

Nicholas Fund started life as the Nicholas Strong Fund, an aggressive growth fund that had no fear of bear markets. The 1973–74 market crash took care of that. These days, Albert Nicholas still looks for companies with the prospect of healthy earnings growth, but he is a buyer only if he can get these companies at modest price/earnings multiple. As a result, this fund, which leans toward medium-sized companies, shows all the hallmarks of a value fund, despite its growth-stock orientation.

Load: None. *Expenses:* 0.76%. *Turnover:* 12%. *Minimum investment:* $500. *Telephone:* 414-272-6133.

Quest for Value Dual Purpose Fund

Quest for Value is an unusual type of closed-end fund known as a dual-purpose fund. For a quick explanation of how these funds work, see the description that accompanies the above listing for Gemini II. Like Gemini II, this fund will liquidate in 1997. Quest's fund manager since 1991, George Long, uses a broad mix of securities, including junk bonds, stocks, money market instruments, and convertible bonds, to try to deliver decent gains to holders of both the income and the capital shares.

Expenses: 0.75%. *Turnover:* 62%. *Stock exchange:* NYSE. *Ticker symbol for capital shares:* KFV. *Ticker symbol for income shares:* KFVpr. *Telephone:* 800-232-3863.

Salomon Brothers Opportunity Fund

Managed by Irving Brilliant, this fund lived up to its manager's name during the 1980s, ranking as the fund industry's 39th-best-performing fund. But that was largely due to sparkling results in the early 1980s. Lately the brilliance has dimmed. In the period 1986–90, the fund lagged the Standard & Poor's 500 stock index in four out of five years. More recently, aided by a big bet on beaten-down financial stocks, Brilliant has shown signs of returning to his old form.

Load: None. *Expenses:* 1.30%. *Turnover:* 11%. *Minimum investment:* $1,000. *Telephone:* 800-725-6666.

Source Capital

This is a closed-end fund. Success can be a terrible thing in the mutual fund industry. High-flying mutual funds tend to attract a lot of money from new investors, making good future performance more difficult. Closed-end funds are immune to that problem; because they have a fixed number of shares outstanding, there's no way for investors to flood a successful manager with heaps of new cash. But closed-end funds can suffer a different symptom of success—premium share prices. That's certainly the case with Source Capital, whose shares consistently trade for more than the fund's underlying per-share portfolio value. The premium is a tribute to the stock-picking prowess of fund manager George Michaelis, who looks for companies that have shown the ability to compound retained profits at a consistently high level. That strategy helped make Source Capital the second-best closed-end stock fund in the 1980s, with a market-beating return of 430.1%. Consider buying this fund—if you can get it at a discount.

Expenses: 0.98%. *Turnover:* 74%. *Stock exchange:* NYSE.
Ticker symbol: SOR. *Telephone:* 310-473-0225/800-982-4372.

Southeastern Asset Management Value Trust

Value managers often say that they like to buy $1 of assets for 50 cents. Southeastern Asset Management's O. Mason Hawkins puts it into practice. An unusually rigorous analyst, he rips apart corporate financial statements to determine a company's true value. He looks for attributes like hidden assets, understated inventories, plentiful cash flow, valuable brand names, and financial assets that are carried on the company's balance sheet for a fraction of their real worth. That strategy has produced good long-term results, though also patches of poor performance, as in 1990, when the fund slumped 16.4%. If you are put off by the fund's $50,000 minimum, consider buying it through your IRA. The minimum initial investment for IRA accounts is $10,000.

Load: None. *Expenses:* 1.29%. *Turnover:* 29%. *Minimum investment:* $50,000. *Telephone:* 901-761-2474/800-445-9469.

T. Rowe Price Equity-Income Fund

Managers Tom Broadus and Brian Rogers, who have run the fund since its 1985 launch, use all the traditional value yardsticks in picking stocks—cash flow, book value, earnings. But as an equity-income fund, probably the most important stock-picking criteria is a stock's dividend yield. The fund aims to have a yield that is somewhat higher than that of the overall market.

Load: None. *Expenses:* 0.97%. *Turnover:* 30%. *Minimum investment:* $2,500. *Telephone:* 410-547-2308/800-638-5660.

Vanguard Equity-Income Fund

Like the folks who run T. Rowe Price Equity-Income, Vanguard Equity-Income Fund's Roger Newell is a "relative yield" buyer. Thus, he doesn't just look for stocks that are yielding more than the market. He also looks at whether a stock's yield relative to the market is at the high end of the stock's historical trading pattern. This fund was launched in 1988, just before value investing went out of favor. Its performance numbers should look a lot better when value investing returns to favor.

Load: None. *Expenses:* 0.44%. *Turnover:* 13%. *Minimum investment:* $3,000. *Telephone:* 215-669-1000/800-662-7447.

Vanguard Windsor II

Despite the name, this fund isn't managed by John Neff, the legendary manager who runs Vanguard's Windsor Fund, which is now closed to new investors. Instead, management of Windsor II falls to four separate portfolio managers, though one of the four managers, James Barrow, currently runs three-quarters of the fund's assets. Low expenses and the use of multiple managers makes this a solid, if somewhat dull, choice for fund investors.

Load: None. *Expenses:* 0.41%. *Turnover:* 23%. *Minimum investment:* $3,000. *Telephone:* 215-669-1000/800-662-7447.

Yacktman Fund

Launched in 1992, this fund is managed by Donald Yacktman, who ran Selected American Shares from 1983 to 1992. Yacktman's stellar reputation is built on his fine performance in the period 1989–91. While most value funds were suffering mightily, Selected American Shares returned 68.8% in that three-year period, compared with 66.3% for the Standard & Poor's 500 stock index. Yacktman's emphasis on top-quality companies that were cheap relative to cash flow helped him avoid some of the cyclical and financial stocks that dragged down other value funds during this period. But just as Yacktman's performance didn't slump when value was out of favor, so his fund may not lead the pack when value investing comes back into vogue.

Load: None. *Expenses:* N.A. *Turnover:* N.A. *Minimum investment:* $5,000. *Telephone:* 312-201-1200/800-525-8258.

Small-company Growth Funds

Brandywine Fund

Brandywine's manager, Foster Friess, is a diehard growth-stock investor with a record rivaled by few others. He set up his own investment advisory firm in 1974 and at the time had just one account, the U.S. stock portfolio of Sweden's Nobel Foundation, which gives out the annual Nobel prizes. Since then, Friess has generated stellar returns first with his private accounts and now with his mutual fund. He relies on a team of in-house analysts who do intensive research on every company bought. The fund isn't restricted to smaller-company stocks, but its search for fast-growing companies leads it toward those sorts of companies. Brandywine Fund's biggest drawback: its hefty $25,000 minimum.

Load: None. *Expenses:* 1.10%. *Turnover:* 189%. *Minimum investment:* $25,000. *Telephone:* 302-656-6200.

Columbia Special Fund

During the late 1980s, when most small-stock funds were suffering, Columbia Special was sparkling. The credit for that good performance goes to manager Alan Folkman's unusual stock-picking strategy. Folkman buys a mix of growth stocks, sector bets, and special situations, allowing him to do well in a variety of market environments. With the exception of 1990, when the fund got bludgeoned for a 12.4% loss, Columbia Special's annual returns have consistently been close to or ahead of the market averages.

Load: None. *Expenses:* 1.19%. *Turnover:* 99%. *Minimum investment:* $2,000. *Telephone:* 503-222-3606/800-547-1707.

Founders Discovery Fund
Founders Frontier Fund

Denver has emerged as a hub for growth-stock fund managers who favor up-and-coming companies with rapid earnings growth. Founders Discovery and Founders Frontier fit right into that mold. Both funds are run by Michael Haines, who has a fondness for high-flying companies but isn't willing to pay up for them. Haines is quick to sell stocks that aren't working out, an approach that is reflected in both funds' rapid portfolio turnover. Founders Discovery leans toward smaller stocks than Founders Frontier, which will likely make Discovery especially prone to bear market batterings.

Founders Discovery Fund—*Load:* None. *Expenses:* 1.97%. *Turnover:* 134%. *Minimum investment:* $1,000. *Telephone:* 303-394-4404/800-525-2440.

Founders Frontier Fund—*Load:* None. *Expenses:* 1.84%. *Turnover:* 171%. *Minimum investment:* $1,000. *Telephone:* 303-394-4404/800-525-2440.

IAI Regional Fund

IAI Regional sticks close to home. By charter, the fund has to keep 80% of its assets in companies from seven Midwestern states: Iowa, Minnesota, Montana, Nebraska, North Dakota, South Dakota, and Wisconsin. The fund, which was launched in 1980, was the 32nd-best-performing fund in the 10 years ended December 1990. Like IAI Stock Fund (see above), IAI Regional is run by Julian "Bing" Carlin. IAI Regional isn't a pure small-stock play. But its strong record and hefty holdings of small-and medium-sized companies make IAI Regional an interesting buy for more conservative investors.

Load: None. *Expenses:* 1.25%. *Turnover:* 141%. *Minimum investment:* $5,000. *Telephone:* 612-376-2600/800-945-3863.

Meridian Fund

Launched in 1984, Richard Aster's Meridian Fund got off to a rocky start, lagging the market badly through its first three years of operation. In 1987 alone, the fund was pounded for a 7.8% loss, while the Standard & Poor's 500 stock index was up over 5%. Recent performance has been much stronger, but investors have yet to notice. The fund remains small, with just $34 million in assets at year-end 1992. Therein lies Meridian's attraction. With many small-company stock funds overflowing with money, Meridian remains an interesting choice for investors looking for a smaller, more nimble small-company growth fund.

Load: None. *Expenses:* 1.59%. *Turnover:* 32%. *Minimum investment:* $2,000. *Telephone:* 415-461-6237/800-446-6662.

Morgan Grenfell Smallcap Fund

A closed-end fund, Morgan Grenfell Smallcap isn't for the faint of heart. This fund has an aggressive growth-stock style, focusing mostly on companies with market values between $50 million and $500 million. In 1994, shareholders will get to vote on whether to turn the fund into an open-end mutual fund, which will have the effect of closing the fund's discount.

Expenses: 1.79%. *Turnover:* 89%. *Stock exchange:* NYSE. *Ticker symbol:* MGC. *Telephone:* 212-230-2600/800-888-8060.

Scudder Development Fund

If small stocks return to favor in the 1990s, as many investment advisers expect, then Scudder Development should be a major beneficiary. Unfortunately, however, thousands of investors have already reached the same conclusion. Scudder Development's assets almost tripled in 1991, turning the fund into one of the country's largest small-stock funds. Manager Roy McKay keeps turnover low, which means the fund's large size may not be an overwhelming problem. Nonetheless, investors may want to look elsewhere.

Load: None. *Expenses:* 1.30%. *Turnover:* 54%. *Minimum investment:* $1,000. *Telephone:* 617-439-4640/800-225-2470.

Sit "New Beginning" Growth Fund

Sit "New Beginning" Growth has all the hallmarks of a top-notch stock fund. This fund has one of the best long-term records of any small-stock fund. Its expenses are low, assets aren't too large, turnover is moderate, and fund manager Douglas Jones has been at the helm since the fund's 1982 launch. While other small-stock growth funds have done somewhat better in recent years, Sit "New Beginning" Growth remains a fine choice.

Load: None. *Expenses:* 0.83%. *Turnover:* 25%. *Minimum investment:* $2,000. *Telephone:* 612-334-5888/800-332-5580.

Strong Common Stock Fund
Strong Opportunity Fund

Since taking over the management of Strong Opportunity Fund in early 1991, stock market veterans Dick Weiss and Carlene Murphy have turned the fund into one of the finest vehicles for investing in mid-sized growth companies. However, for Weiss and Murphy, this isn't their first mutual fund success. The stock-picking duo made their names as managers of SteinRoe Special Fund, which posted sparkling returns during the 1980s. They have also garnered attention for the fine performance of Strong Common Stock Fund, a small-company stock fund that was closed to new investors in early 1993. With all these funds, Weiss and Murphy have used intensive company-by-company research to root out fast-growing corporations whose stocks are trading at low multiples of earnings.

Load: None. *Expenses:* 1.60%. *Turnover:* 170%. *Minimum investment:* $1,000. *Telephone:* 414-359-1400/800-368-1030.

T. Rowe Price New Horizons Fund

The granddaddy of small-stock funds, T. Rowe Price New Horizons can frolic like a young kid when growth stocks are booming. For proof of that, take a look at 1991's dazzling 52.2% gain. But with more than $1 billion in assets, there is a limit to how nimble this fund can be. As with Scudder Development and Twentieth Century Ultra, investors should probably look elsewhere.

Load: None. *Expenses:* 0.93%. *Turnover:* 50%. *Minimum investment:* $2,500. *Telephone:* 410-547-2308/800-638-5660.

Twentieth Century Giftrust Investors
Twentieth Century Ultra Investors
Twentieth Century Vista Investors

Like Twentieth Century's large-company growth funds (see above), these three funds use a hard-driving growth-stock style. Ultra has the best record, but investors have woken up to that fact: Ultra already has more than $5 billion in assets. Giftrust is much smaller, in large part because it is designed to be used by those who want to make a gift to a charity or to another person. Vista, meanwhile, has the poorest record of the three funds, but it may actually be the best bet. It is substantially smaller than Ultra and it doesn't have the restrictions on investor purchases that apply to Giftrust. And going forward, Vista will have the benefit of the same computer-driven stock selection system that has generated great returns at the other Twentieth Century funds.

Twentieth Century Giftrust Investors—*Load:* None. *Expenses:* 1.00%. *Turnover:* 134%. *Minimum investment:* $250. *Telephone:* 816-531-5575/800-345-2021.

Twentieth Century Ultra Investors—*Load:* None. *Expenses:* 1.00%. *Turnover:* 59%. *Minimum investment:* None. *Telephone:* 816-531-5575/800-345-2021.

Twentieth Century Vista Investors—*Load:* None. *Expenses:* 1.00%. *Turnover:* 87%. *Minimum investment:* None. *Telephone:* 816-531-5575/800-345-2021.

Small-company Value Funds

Babson Enterprise Fund II

This fund is run by Peter Schliemann, who carved a name for himself as manager of the Babson Enterprise Fund. The original Enterprise Fund was closed to new investors in early 1992, but the sequel promises to be just as good. Babson Enterprise II uses the same stock-picking strategy as the original Enterprise Fund, except that Enterprise II buys somewhat larger stocks. Schliemann, who looks for rapidly growing companies that have fallen from favor, has emerged as one of the finest small-stock value managers. This fund is a buy.

Load: None. *Expenses:* 1.83%. *Turnover:* 14%. *Minimum investment:* $1,000. *Telephone:* 816-471-5200/800-422-2766.

Evergreen Limited Market Fund

Like so many other managers, Evergreen Limited Market Fund's Robin Kelly tries to buy fast-growing companies that are priced at low multiples of expected earnings. So how does Kelly get her edge? She dabbles in so-called micro-cap stocks, tiny companies with stock market values of less than $100 million that tend to get overlooked by other stockpickers. Kelly, who has run the fund since its mid-1983 launch, has one of the fund industry's best records. Despite that stellar performance, the Evergreen Fund has remained small, in large part because the fund was closed to new investors for much of its first nine years of operation.

Load: None. *Expenses:* 1.25%. *Turnover:* 55%. *Minimum investment:* $5,000. *Telephone:* 914-694-2020/800-235-0064.

Fasciano Fund

Fund manager Michael Fasciano looks for fast-growing companies trading at below-average earnings multiples. He prefers firms with stock market values below $500 million that are not widely followed by Wall Street analysts. Fasciano's conservative growth-stock strategy is somewhat reminiscent of the style of Albert Nicholas, who runs Nicholas Fund and Nicholas II. Maybe that's no great surprise: Nicholas is Fasciano's father-in-law.

Load: None. *Expenses:* 1.70%. *Turnover:* 29%. *Minimum investment:* $1,000. *Telephone:* 312-444-6050/800-848-6050.

GIT Equity Trust–Special Growth Portfolio

At the start of 1990, GIT Equity Trust–Special Growth ranked as the third-best-performing small-stock fund for the prior five years. But for manager Richard Carney, there followed two miserable years; the fund slumped badly in 1990 and then recovered only modestly in 1991. Carney's approach, which emphasizes undervalued companies with low debt and sustainable earnings growth, should generate decent long-term returns. But after the fund's rotten performance in 1990 and 1991, it's understandable if investors are leery of this fund.

Load: None. *Expenses:* 1.36%. *Turnover:* 24%. *Minimum investment:* $2,500. *Telephone:* 703-528-6500/800-336-3063.

Lazard Special Equity Portfolio

This fund can't quite match Babson Enterprise in the five-year performance rankings. But it shows an edge in years like 1987 and 1990, when small-stock funds got beaten up. For those who can afford the $50,000 minimum, this is one of the better choices among small-stock value funds.

Load: None. *Expenses:* 1.70%. *Turnover:* 11%. *Minimum investment:* $50,000. *Telephone:* 212-632-6000/800-228-0203.

Neuberger & Berman Genesis Fund

Like Neuberger & Berman's other offerings, Genesis offers a prudent way to invest in value stocks. The fund probably won't ever rank as a top performer, but it is also unlikely to disappoint. The only obvious drawback is the fund's high annual expenses.

Load: None. *Expenses:* 2.00%. *Turnover:* 23%. *Minimum investment:* $1,000. *Telephone:* 212-476-8800/800-877-9700.

Nicholas II

Like Nicholas Fund (see page 183), Nicholas II has the benefit of the investment talents of Albert Nicholas. Ab Nicholas rarely advertises, his company doesn't have a toll-free number for prospective investors, and his downtown Milwaukee offices are a stark reminder that mutual funds were once a financial backwater. But despite Nicholas's low-key approach to business, his funds have started to garner more and more attention from investors. Nicholas II's assets have grown steadily, crossing the $500 million mark in 1991. As a result, it has become tougher for the fund to take significant positions in the stocks of very small companies. Even with that caveat, this fund has a lot to recommend it.

Load: None. *Expenses:* 0.66%. *Turnover:* 12%. *Minimum investment:* $1,000. *Telephone:* 414-272-6133.

Pennsylvania Mutual Fund

Managed by Charles Royce and Thomas Ebright since the 1970s, Pennsylvania Mutual buys shares of some of the smallest companies in the small-stock universe. The fund's strict application of value criteria dampens the fund's share-price gyrations, so that it offers a remarkably smooth ride for a small-stock fund. The fund's growing size—its assets recently hit $1 billion—is a worry. But because the fund does relatively little trading, that size is less of a problem than it would be for a similarly sized small-company growth fund.

Load: None, though 1% redemption fee charged on shares sold within a year of purchase. *Expenses:* 0.91%. *Turnover:* 35%. *Minimum investment:* $2,000. *Telephone:* 212-355-7311/ 800-221-4268.

Royce Value Trust

This is a closed-end fund. Like Pennsylvania Mutual Fund (see above), this fund is managed by Chuck Royce and Tom Ebright. Over time, Royce Value Trust should tend to outperform Pennsylvania Mutual, partly because of lower annual expenses. In addition, unlike Pennsylvania Mutual, the closed-end Royce Value Trust doesn't have to hold cash in order to meet shareholder redemptions. That cash acts as a drag on Pennsylvania Mutual's performance.

Expenses: 0.68%. *Turnover:* 48%. *Stock exchange:* NYSE. *Ticker symbol:* RVT. *Telephone:* 212-355-7311/800-221-4268.

International Stock Funds

Acorn International

Launched in late 1992, Acorn International is run by Ralph Wanger, the long-time manager of Acorn Fund, a top-ranked small-company stock fund that is now closed to new investors. In recent years, Acorn Fund has invested a growing chunk of its assets in foreign small-company stocks. With Acorn International, which invests exclusively in foreign small-company stocks, Wanger aims to exploit the international stock-picking skills he has developed while running Acorn Fund. Buyers of Acorn International should consider combining it with a fund that invests in larger foreign-company stocks.

Load: None. *Expenses:* N.A. *Turnover:* N.A. *Minimum investment:* $1,000. *Telephone:* 800-922-6769.

Babson-Stewart Ivory International Fund

Managed by John Wright of Stewart Ivory & Co., in Edinburgh, Scotland, this fund has done somewhat better than the average international fund in each of the last few years. Unlike other foreign-stock fund managers, Wright leans toward medium-and small-sized stocks, and the fund has some exposure to emerging markets. That, plus the fund's small size, makes it an intriguing buy.

Load: None. *Expenses:* 1.58%. *Turnover:* 44%. *Minimum investment:* $2,500. *Telephone:* 816-471-5200/800-422-2766.

Harbor International Fund

Hakan Castegren is emerging as one of the premier global stock-pickers. A value investor whose investment style seems almost eccentric, Castegren has a blanket prohibition on investing in Germany, and he says he won't buy defense, high technology, or drug stocks. He is also intensely secretive about what he is buying or selling at any one time. All that said, the fund's results are hard to argue with. If you want to invest abroad, consider using this fund.

Load: None. *Expenses:* 1.28%. *Turnover:* 25%. *Minimum investment:* $2,000. *Telephone:* 419-247-2477/800-422-1050.

Montgomery Emerging Markets Fund

It is always preferable to buy a fund with at least a five-year record, but sometimes you have to break the rules. Emerging markets funds are a recent phenomena. The oldest of the group, Templeton Emerging Markets Fund, has been around only since 1987. If you can buy the Templeton fund at a discount, it's probably the best bet in the group. But the Templeton fund has regularly traded at a premium and, in any case, you may not want to dabble in closed-end funds. If that's the case, consider Montgomery Emerging Markets Fund, a no-load mutual fund launched in 1992. Its managers, Bryan Sudweeks and Josephine Jimenez, have been investing in emerging markets since 1988. They combine a computer-driven strategy that determines how much money they allocate to each country with a more traditional, fundamental analysis of each individual stock that they buy.

Load: None, though 2% redemption fee charged if shares held for less than a year. *Expenses:* 1.90%. *Turnover:* N.A. *Minimum investment:* $2,000. *Telephone:* 415-627-2400/800-428-1871.

Morgan Stanley Emerging Markets Fund

This closed-end Morgan Stanley fund was launched only in late 1991, so that—as with Montgomery Emerging Markets Fund—investors who purchase the fund are buying partly on faith. But buyers of the Morgan Stanley fund do have a way of stacking the odds in their favor. If they can buy the fund at a big discount, that should provide a buffer in case the fund's management turns out to be less than stellar. Morgan Stanley Emerging Markets uses a top-down approach. The fund starts out by allocating money to those countries whose markets seem cheapest. The stock selection is then left to the Morgan Stanley analyst who is responsible for that country.

Expenses: 2.10%. *Turnover:* N.A. *Stock exchange:* NYSE. *Ticker symbol:* MSF. *Telephone:* 212-296-7100/800-221-6726.

Scudder International Fund

Like T. Rowe Price Associates, Scudder Funds has a solid reputation for international investing. In keeping with that reputation, Scudder International Fund has posted decent, but not spectacular, long-term results. The fund's allocation among different countries is driven by consideration of both macroeconomic factors and the merits of individual companies. While most foreign-stock funds have a bias toward growth stocks, Scudder International is more value oriented.

Load: None. *Expenses:* 1.26%. *Turnover:* 34%. *Minimum investment:* $1,000. *Telephone:* 617-439-4640/800-225-2470.

T. Rowe Price International Discovery Fund

Unlike most international stock funds, with their predictable mix of large-company stocks, T. Rowe Price International Discovery ventures far from the beaten path. The fund owns a mix of small- and medium-sized stocks from developed countries and from emerging markets. While this fund is riskier than most foreign-stock funds, it should be viewed as a conservative alternative to a pure emerging markets fund. Like an emerging markets fund, T. Rowe Price International Discovery should be owned in combination with a foreign-stock fund that emphasizes bigger stocks from developed markets.

Load: None. *Expenses:* 1.50%. *Turnover:* 38%. *Minimum investment:* $2,500. *Telephone:* 410-547-2308/800-638-5660.

T. Rowe Price International Stock Fund

Among larger fund groups, T. Rowe Price Associates has emerged as possibly the finest manager of foreign-stock funds. T. Rowe Price International Stock Fund is the group's flagship fund. Launched in 1980, it has one of the best long-term records among all foreign-stock funds. It uses a top-down approach that involves making decisions on what countries, currencies, and industry sectors seem attractive.

Load: None. *Expenses:* 1.05%. *Turnover:* 38%. *Minimum investment:* $2,500. *Telephone:* 410-547-2308/800-638-5660.

Templeton Emerging Markets Fund

This is a closed-end fund. Almost single-handedly, Templeton Emerging Markets manager Mark Mobius has proved the value of investing in emerging markets. In the five years following its March 1987 launch, the fund returned 226.7%, compared with just 63.9% for the Standard & Poor's 500 stock index. Like the rest of the Templeton funds, Mobius takes a strict value approach, avoiding top-down analysis and instead focusing on the virtues of individual stocks. Templeton Emerging Markets rarely trades at a discount, so buyers have to be patient.

Expenses: 1.91%. *Turnover:* 53%. *Stock exchange:* NYSE. *Ticker symbol:* EMF. *Telephone:* 813-823-8712/800-237-0738.

Vanguard Trustees' Commingled Fund–International Portfolio

Vanguard Trustees' International goes strictly by the numbers. The fund is run using a computer-driven stock selection system, which makes it a rarity in the foreign-stock fund arena. Jarrod Wilcox took over the fund's management in 1991. But Wilcox isn't a newcomer to the fund. He had also managed Vanguard Trustees' International from 1984 to 1985, before leaving to work for Colonial Management. The fund typically buys smaller stocks that look cheap on value criteria. Wilcox doesn't hedge the fund's currency exposure.

Load: None. *Expenses:* 0.43%. *Turnover:* 56%. *Minimum investment:* $10,000. *Telephone:* 215-669-1000/800-662-7447.

Vanguard World Fund–International Growth Portfolio

Most foreign-stock fund managers stick with tried-and-true blue-chip stocks. Not Richard Foulkes. He looks for companies with rapid earnings growth that are at low price-to-earnings multiples compared to other stocks in their particular national stock market. This search for undervalued growth stocks often leads Foulkes to buy the stocks of smaller companies. Foulkes, who has run the fund since 1981, has put together a strong long-term track record. Recent results have, however, been less than stellar.

Load: None. *Expenses:* 0.58%. *Turnover:* 58%. *Minimum investment:* $3,000. *Telephone:* 215-669-1000/800-662-7447.

Warburg Pincus International Equity Fund

Though a relative newcomer to the international stock fund arena, Warburg Pincus International Equity Fund has already started garnering attention. In 1990, the fund's first full calendar year, fund manager Richard King kept losses to 4.6%, while foreign-stock funds were hit with average losses of 11.2%. In 1991, when foreign-stock funds gained just 13.2%, the Warburg fund jumped 20.6%. King has a preference for rapidly growing companies and economies, which leads him to keep a large percentage of the fund's assets in emerging markets.

Load: None. *Expenses:* 1.50%. *Turnover:* 53%. *Minimum investment:* $2,500. *Telephone:* 212-878-0600/800-888-6878.

Stock Index Funds

Dreyfus Peoples Index Fund
Fidelity Market Index Fund
Vanguard Index Trust–500 Portfolio

All three funds invest in companies that comprise the Standard & Poor's 500 stock index, a benchmark index that is dominated by the stocks of larger companies. In buying an index fund, expenses should be the key consideration. On that score, Vanguard has the edge, though other funds may occasionally boast lower costs because they are temporarily absorbing all or part of their expenses. To index the entire U.S. market, combine one of these S&P 500 funds with Vanguard Index Trust–Extended Market Portfolio.

Dreyfus Peoples Index Fund—*Load:* None, though 1% redemption fee charged if shares sold within six months of purchase. *Expenses:* N.A. *Turnover:* 3%. *Minimum investment:* $2,500. *Telephone:* 718-895-1206/800-645-6561.

Fidelity Market Index Fund—*Load:* None, though 0.5% redemption fee charged if shares sold within six months of purchase. *Expenses:* 0.43%. *Turnover:* 0%. *Minimum investment:* $2,500. *Telephone:* 800-544-8888.

Vanguard Index Trust–500 Portfolio—*Load:* None. *Expenses:* 0.19%. *Turnover:* 4%. *Minimum investment:* $3,000. *Telephone:* 215-669-1000/800-662-7447.

Dreyfus Peoples S&P MidCap Index Fund

The Dreyfus MidCap Fund seeks to replicate the performance of S&P MidCap 400 Index, which includes 400 mid-sized U.S. companies that are not in the Standard & Poor's 500 stock index. Buying both the Dreyfus MidCap Fund and an S&P 500 fund would allow you to index much of the U.S. stock market. But if you are looking to index the entire U.S. market, it makes more sense to combine an S&P 500 fund with Vanguard's Extended Market Portfolio, because you will end up owning a broader group of stocks.

Load: None, though 1% redemption fee charged if shares sold within six months. *Expenses:* N.A. *Turnover:* N.A. *Minimum investment:* $2,500. *Telephone:* 718-895-1206/800-645-6561.

Schwab 1000 Fund

The Schwab 1000 Fund invests in the 1,000 largest publicly traded U.S. companies, as measured by market capitalization. This means the fund owns a mixture of large and medium-sized companies. But because the largest 500 companies account for the bulk of the fund's assets, the Schwab fund will tend to have similar performance to S&P 500 index funds.

Load: None, though 0.5% redemption fee charged if shares sold within six months of purchase. *Expenses:* N.A. *Turnover:* N.A. *Minimum investment:* $1,000. *Telephone:* 800-526-8600.

Vanguard Index Trust–Extended Market Portfolio

This fund seeks to track the performance of the Wilshire 4500, an index of small and medium-sized stocks that includes all U.S. stocks outside of the Standard & Poor's 500 stock index. To index the entire U.S. stock market, this fund should be coupled with an S&P 500 index fund.

Load: None, though fund charges a 1% transaction fee that is paid to the fund. *Expenses:* 0.20% *Turnover:* 9%. *Minimum investment:* $3,000. *Telephone:* 215-669-1000/800-662-7447.

Vanguard Index Trust–Total Stock Market Portfolio

The Total Stock Market Portfolio tries to replicate the performance of the entire U.S. stock market, as measured by the Wilshire 5000. If you want to index the entire U.S. market, this fund is the way to go.

Load: None, though fund charges a 0.25% transaction fee that is paid to the fund. *Expenses:* 0.21%. *Turnover:* N.A. *Minimum investment:* $3,000. *Telephone:* 215-669-1000/800-662-7447.

Vanguard International Equity Index Fund– European Portfolio

Launched in 1990, Vanguard's European index fund seeks to replicate the performance of the Morgan Stanley Capital International Europe Index. If this fund is combined—in the right proportions—with Vanguard's Pacific Portfolio, an investor can match the performance of the Morgan Stanley Capital International Index for Europe, Australia, and the Far East. Neither the European Portfolio nor the Pacific Portfolio use hedging techniques to reduce their foreign currency exposure; as a result, the rise and fall of the dollar can have a powerful impact on both funds' results.

Load: None, though fund charges a 1% transaction fee that is paid to the fund. *Expenses:* 0.31%. *Turnover:* 1%. *Minimum investment:* $3,000. *Telephone:* 215-669-1000/800-662-7447.

Vanguard International Equity Index Fund–Pacific Portfolio

Vanguard's Pacific index fund seeks to track the performance of the Morgan Stanley Capital International Pacific Index. The index includes stocks from Australia, Hong Kong, and Singapore, but the biggest component by far is Japan. As a result, this fund's results are driven by the whims of the Tokyo stock market. In 1992, that meant atrocious performance.

Load: None, though fund charges a 1% transaction fee that

is paid to the fund. *Expenses:* 0.30%. *Turnover:* 0%. *Minimum investment:* $3,000. *Telephone:* 215-669-1000/800-662-7447.

Vanguard Small Capitalization Stock Fund

In an earlier life, this fund was known as the Naess & Thomas Special Fund. Its performance was anything but special, so in 1989 Vanguard converted it into an index fund. The fund buys the stocks in the Russell 2000 stock index and thereby hopes to match the index's performance. The Russell 2000, a small-stock index, has a much lower average market capitalization than either the Wilshire 4500 or the Standard & Poor's MidCap Index. Like the Dreyfus MidCap Fund, the Vanguard Small Capitalization Stock Fund can be used in conjunction with an S&P 500 fund, thereby giving investors exposure to much of the U.S. stock market. But if your aim is to get exposure to all U.S. stocks, you would be better off with either the Vanguard Total Stock Market Portfolio or a combination of an S&P 500 fund and Vanguard's Extended Market Portfolio.

Load: None, though fund charges a 1% transaction fee that is paid to the fund. *Expenses:* 0.18%. *Turnover:* 26%. *Minimum investment:* $3,000. *Telephone:* 215-669-1000/800-662-7447.

Bond Funds

Fidelity Global Bond Fund
Scudder International Bond Fund
T. Rowe Price International Bond Fund

Because the T. Rowe Price fund invests almost exclusively abroad, it bounces around fairly sharply in share price. But T. Rowe Price International Bond is your best bet if you want a pure play on foreign bonds. By contrast, the Fidelity and Scudder funds will usually have some U.S. bond exposure, which makes them less volatile. Fidelity Global Bond Fund, in particular, has tended to keep a significant portion of its portfolio in U.S. bonds.

Fidelity Global Bond Fund—*Load:* None. *Expenses:* 1.37%. *Minimum investment:* $2,500. *Telephone:* 800-544-8888.

Scudder International Bond Fund—*Load:* None. *Expenses:* 1.25%. *Minimum investment:* $1,000. *Telephone:* 617-439-4640/800-225-2470.

T. Rowe Price International Bond Fund—*Load:* None. *Expenses:* 1.10%. *Minimum investment:* $2,500. *Telephone:* 410-547-2308/800-638-5660.

Fidelity Short-Term Bond Portfolio
Neuberger & Berman Limited Maturity Bond Fund
Scudder Short-Term Bond Fund
Vanguard Short-Term Corporate Portfolio

Any of these short-term bond funds would be a good place to park any emergency money you might have. Short-term bond funds typically offer significantly higher yields than money market funds, but shareholders usually suffer only modest share price fluctuations. The Vanguard fund has the advantage of rock-bottom expenses. Some of the other funds have bolstered returns by either dabbling in riskier securities or temporarily holding down expenses. A word of warning: Short-term bond funds typically allow shareholders to write checks against their accounts. Think carefully before doing this. If you write a check against your bond fund, you will end up taking a capital gain or loss, which you then have to report on your tax return.

Fidelity Short-Term Bond Portfolio—*Load:* None. *Expenses:* 0.75%. *Minimum investment:* $2,500. *Telephone:* 800-544-8888.

Neuberger & Berman Limited Maturity Bond Fund—*Load:* None. *Expenses:* 0.65%. *Minimum investment:* $5,000. *Telephone:* 212-476-8800/800-877-9700.

Scudder Short-Term Bond Fund—*Load:* None. *Expenses:* 0.78%. *Minimum investment:* $1,000. *Telephone:* 617-439-4640/800-225-2470.

Vanguard Short-Term Corporate Portfolio—*Load:* None. *Expenses:* 0.30%. *Minimum investment:* $3,000. *Telephone:* 215-669-1000/800-662-7447.

Fidelity Spartan High-Income Fund
Financial Funds–High Yield Portfolio
Nicholas Income Fund
T. Rowe Price High-Yield Fund
Vanguard High-Yield Portfolio

These five funds are among the more conservative junk bond funds. The offerings from Financial Funds, Nicholas, and Vanguard are especially risk-adverse. All of the funds have long and distinguished track records, with the exception of Fidelity Spartan High-Income Fund, which was launched only in 1990. But the Fidelity fund's manager, Margaret Eagle, has produced strong results with Fidelity Advisor High-Yield Portfolio, another junk bond fund that she manages. The Fidelity Advisor fund, which was launched in early 1987, is sold through brokers and charges a 4.75% upfront sales commission, so investors are better off buying the no-load Fidelity Spartan High-Income Fund.

Fidelity Spartan High-Income Fund—*Load:* None, though 1% redemption fee charged if shares sold within nine months of purchase. *Expenses:* 0.70% *Minimum investment:* $10,000. *Telephone:* 800-544-8888.

Financial Funds–High Yield Portfolio—*Load:* None. *Expenses:* 1.05%. *Minimum investment:* $1,000. *Telephone:* 303-930-6300/800-525-8085.

Nicholas Income Fund—*Load:* None. *Expenses:* 0.66%. *Minimum investment:* $500. *Telephone:* 414-272-6133.

T. Rowe Price High-Yield Fund—*Load:* None. *Expenses:* 0.89%. *Minimum investment:* $2,500. *Telephone:* 410-547-2308/800-638-5660.

Vanguard High-Yield Portfolio—*Load:* None. *Expenses:* 0.36%. *Minimum investment:* $3,000. *Telephone:* 215-669-1000/800-662-7447.

Harbor Bond Fund
PIMCO Total Return Fund

Both of these funds are managed by William Gross, one of the country's best bond fund managers. Investors who can't afford PIMCO Total Return Portfolio's $500,000 minimum can get into the fund for just $1,000 if they go through Charles Schwab & Co., the San Francisco discount brokerage firm. Schwab charges a small transaction fee for its services. Because PIMCO's expenses are lower than Harbor's, it may be worth paying that transaction fee, provided you plan to hang on to the fund for more than a couple of years.

Harbor Bond Fund—*Load:* None. *Expenses:* 0.77%. *Minimum investment:* $2,000. *Telephone:* 419-247-2477/800-422-1050.

PIMCO Total Return Fund—*Load:* None. *Expenses:* 0.42%. *Minimum investment:* $500,000. *Telephone:* 800-927-4648.

T. Rowe Price Spectrum Income Fund

Spectrum Income makes its money by buying seven other T. Rowe Price funds that are income oriented, including the Baltimore fund group's junk bond fund, international bond fund, taxable money market fund, Ginnie Mae fund, high-quality bond fund, short-term bond fund, and equity-income fund. For investors, Spectrum Income provides an easy and relatively inexpensive way of getting a diversified bond fund portfolio. The fund itself charges no annual expenses. Investors do, however, end up paying the fees of the other T. Rowe Price funds that are bought. This fund should be viewed as a somewhat imperfect substitute for the three-fund strategy described at the end of chapter 16.

Load: None. *Expenses:* N.A. *Minimum investment:* $2,500. *Telephone:* 410-547-2308/800-638-5660.

Vanguard Bond Market Fund.

Stock index funds have consistently proved their ability to beat the average fund. But within the world of index funds, the real star is a bond fund, Vanguard Bond Market Fund. Helped by its minuscule expenses, Vanguard Bond Market has managed to consistently outpace the majority of its bond fund competitors. The Vanguard fund tries to replicate the performance of the Salomon Brothers Broad Investment-Grade Bond Index. The bulk of the fund's assets are invested in a variety of government bonds, with a smaller portion in corporate bonds. The fund has an average maturity of around 10 years, so the fund is more volatile than a short-term bond fund.

Load: None. *Expenses:* 0.20%. *Minimum investment:* $3,000. *Telephone:* 215-669-1000/800-662-7447.

Glossary

Aggressive Growth Funds. See **Capital Appreciation Funds.**

Balanced Funds. These funds own a mix of stocks and bonds. Many of these funds maintain fixed allocations, usually 60% stocks and 40% bonds, but some funds vary the percentages depending on whether the fund's manager thinks stocks are cheap or expensive.

Capital Appreciation Funds. Also known as aggressive growth funds. These funds are managed for maximum capital gains. Often the funds will trade heavily, make big moves between stocks and cash, and use sophisticated investment techniques, such as the use of leverage or the purchase of options. Most capital appreciation funds are run by managers who use the growth-stock investing style.

Capital Gains Distributions. Though bond and money market funds can make capital gains distributions, you are most likely to get these distributions if you own a stock fund. Funds are compelled by law to pay out virtually all the capital gains they realize each year, unless the fund has more losing trades than winning trades. Most stock funds make a single annual capital gains distribution, in late December, though some stock funds make a second annual distribution, typically in June or July.

Closed-end Funds. Also known as exchange-traded funds and publicly traded funds. Unlike regular mutual funds, closed-end funds have a fixed number of shares outstanding, which trade on the stock exchange. These shares can trade for more or less than the fund's net asset value. If the fund's shares trade for less than its net asset value, the fund is at a discount. If the shares trade for more than the net asset value, the fund is at a premium.

Dollar Cost Averaging. One of the simplest but most effective stock market investment techniques, dollar cost averaging involves investing a fixed amount on a regular basis, such as every month or every three months. In periods when the market is high, your money will buy fewer shares. Conversely, if the market is in a slump your investment will purchase more shares. Because stock prices rise over time, you should eventually own shares that are worth far more than the amount you invested.

Equity-income Funds. Among the more conservative stock funds, equity-income funds tend to pay out big income distributions each year. That income is earned either by buying bonds or by buying high-dividend-paying stocks. Equity-income funds tend to be run by value managers.

Exchange-traded Funds. See **Closed-end Funds.**

Expense Ratio. A fund's expenses in any one year are expressed as a percentage of average fund assets for that period. This expense ratio is usually published in the first few pages of a fund's prospectus. The expense ratio includes costs like fund manager salaries, shareholder servicing expenses, and 12b-1 fees.

Global Funds. These funds invest in both U.S. and foreign stocks. Investors looking for pure foreign exposure may instead want to stick with international funds, which invest exclusively abroad.

Growth-and-income Funds. Like equity-income funds, growth-and-income funds typically buy dividend-paying stocks. But growth-and-income funds aren't quite as income oriented as equity-income funds. Growth-and-income funds are usually managed by value managers.

Growth Funds. The term "growth fund" is used in two different ways. As used by mutual fund companies and by fund researchers like Lipper Analytical Services and Morningstar, Inc., growth funds are those funds that buy stocks that have the potential for above-average earnings growth.

The expression "growth fund" is also used to connote a particular investment style. Growth-stock investors typically buy rapidly growing companies, which may have modest or no current earnings but the potential for fabulous future earnings. Growth stocks often pay out little or nothing in the way of dividends, and these stocks are often richly valued compared to the rest of the market.

Growth-stock funds may be categorized as "growth funds" by Lipper or Morningstar, but they can also appear in other categories. Conversely, some funds that use the value investing style are classified as "growth funds" by Lipper and Morningstar.

High-yield Funds. Also known as junk bond funds. High-yield funds are generally considered the riskiest of all bond funds, because they buy the bonds of companies that could default on their interest payments. To compensate investors for taking that risk, junk bonds generally kick off more income than any other type of bond. Because of bond defaults, there is often a sharp discrepancy between a fund's yield and its total return, which reflects both the dividends paid out by the fund and any change in a fund's share price.

Income Distributions. Every calendar year, mutual funds are compelled by law to pay out virtually all the income and all the capital gains they have earned during that year. Interest earned from owning bonds and dividends earned from owning stocks are included in the income distributions. Bond and money market funds typically make income distributions every month, while a stock fund may only make a single income distribution each year, at the end of December.

Index Funds. An index fund tries to replicate the performance of a particular market index, such as the Standard & Poor's 500 or the Russell 2000. To do that, an index fund buys all or most of the securities that make up the market index that the fund is trying to mimic.

International Funds. Unlike global funds, which hold some U.S. stocks, international funds invest exclusively in foreign stocks.

Junk Bond Funds. See **High-yield Funds.**

Large-company Stock Funds. These funds buy companies with stock market values of $1 billion and up. Fund researchers like Lipper Analytical Services and Morningstar, Inc., typically classify funds that buy larger-company stocks as equity-income funds, growth-and-income funds, growth funds, capital appreciation funds, or aggressive growth funds.

Load. See **Sales Commission.**

Money Market Funds. First offered in the early 1970s, money market funds buy Treasury bills and high-quality corporate commercial paper that will mature within a few months. These funds are considered the safest of all mutual funds. Their shares are pegged at a fixed price, normally $1.

Net Asset Value. This is the formal name given to a fund's share price. It measures the value of the fund's portfolio holdings on a per-share basis.

No-load. The Securities and Exchange Commission defines a no-load fund as one that doesn't charge an upfront or back-end sales commission and doesn't charge a 12b-1 fee of more than 0.25% a year.

Publicly Traded Funds. See **Closed-end Funds.**

Sales Charge. See **Sales Commission.**

Sales Commission. Also known as a sales charge or load. Some funds charge sales commissions either when you buy shares (a front-end load) or when you sell (a back-end load). These commissions are usually used to compensate brokers. But some funds that aren't sold through brokers, such as those managed by Fidelity Investments and Dreyfus Corp., also charge sales commissions. Loads can run as high as 8.5% but in recent years have been reduced. The reduction of front-end and back-end loads has, however, been accompanied by the introduction of 12b-1 fees. Like sales commissions, 12b-1 fees are sometimes used to compensate brokers.

Sector Funds. A sector fund invests in the stocks of a single industry sector, such as health care, technology, or gold.

Short-term Bond Funds. Among the safest of all bond funds, short-term bond funds invest in bonds with less than five years until they mature.

Small-company Stock Funds. These funds buy companies with stock market values of below $1 billion. Fund researchers Lipper Analytical Services and Morningstar, Inc., have a special category for small-company stock funds, though funds that invest largely in small-company stocks are sometimes slotted into other fund categories.

Total Return. A fund's total return reflects not only the income and capital gains distributions that a fund pays out, but also any change in the fund's share price. Total return is the true return earned by a fund shareholder. It can differ sharply from a fund's yield. Total return can be expressed on an annualized or a cumulative basis. If a fund had tripled shareholders' money over the past 10 years, the fund's cumulative 10-year total return would be 200% and its 10-year annualized return would be 11.6%. In this example, the cumulative return is more than 10 times the annualized return because of the way compounding works.

Turnover. A fund's turnover reflects the amount of buying and selling of securities that it does in any one year. If a stock fund has 100% turnover, over the past year the fund has bought and sold stock equal to the entire size of the fund's portfolio, implying an average holding period of one year. Funds with turnover above 100% hold stocks for less than a year, while funds with turnover below 100% hang on to stocks for longer than 12 months.

12b-1 Fees. Introduced in the early 1980s, 12b-1 fees are used by funds to pay for marketing and distribution costs. They have emerged as an alternative method of paying brokers who sell mutual funds. These days, many broker-sold funds will charge both a front-end or back-end sales commission and a 12b-1 fee. In addition, some no-load funds charge a 12b-1 fee, which is used to pay for things like fund advertising. The Securities and Exchange Commission considers a fund to be no-load if it doesn't charge a front-end or back-end sales commission and it has a 12b-1 fee of 0.25% or less.

Value Funds. There is no Lipper Analytical Services or Morningstar, Inc., category known as value. Rather, value is an investment style, and it is usually contrasted with the growth-stock investment style. Value investors typically buy stocks that are cheap relative to earnings, corporate assets, and cash flow; they tend to favor stocks with high dividend yields.

Yield. A fund's yield is the amount of income it kicks off, expressed on an annual basis. Many bond fund investors make the mistake of buying based on yield alone. Because of share price gains or losses, a fund's total return can be substantially different from its yield.

Index